# WHAT
# DOES IT
# PROFIT...?

Christian Dialogue on the U.S. Economy

# WHAT DOES IT PROFIT...?

Shantilal P. Bhagat
with
T. Wayne Reiman
and
Murray L. Wagner, Jr.

The Brethren Press, Elgin, Illinois

# WHAT DOES IT PROFIT . . . ?

*Copyright © 1983 by The Brethren Press*

**Library of Congress Cataloging in Publication Data**

Bhagat, Shantilal P., 1923-
  What does it profit . . . ?

        1. Economics—Religious aspects—Christianity—Addresses,
essays, lectures. 2. United States—Economic conditions—
1971-    —Addresses, essays, lectures. 3. United States—
Economic policy—1981-    —Addresses, essays, lectures.
I. Rieman, T. Wayne.        II. Wagner, Murray L., 1937-
III. Title.
BF115.E3B47    1983        261.8'5'0973        83-3687

**ISBN 0-87178-927-2**

The Brethren Press
1451 Dundee Ave.
Elgin, Ill.
60120

# Contents

# 1
# Christians Look
# at Economics

A cursory glance at the newspapers or a casual tuning into a news broadcast cannot but leave one with the impression that something is seriously wrong with the United States economy. The unemployment rate has reached the highest ever in the past four decades, putting over twelve million people out of work. Prices have been quick to go up but seldom come down. The basic industries (auto, steel, glass, oil, rubber), which in the past played a major role in creating an unprecedented prosperity are on a steady decline. Scores of industrial plants close down or relocate. The number of business failures and bankruptcies keep escalating. Poverty, hunger, and homelessness are on the rise. Wall Street is constantly gyrating. The U.S. Federal government, deep in debt (over a trillion dollars) and unable to discipline or control the three-trillion-dollar economy, grasps to come up with an acceptable federal budget. The state and local governments face serious financial problems and are increasingly unable to meet the aspirations of the citizens. Other social institutions experience economic duress. Communities are destroyed. Families get uprooted, live under anxieties as never before, and are torn apart unable to figure out what is going on. Individuals encounter personal crises and serious problems due to economic hardships and threats of unemployment. There seems to be no end in sight nor any sign of hope for a quick turn-around of the economy much less a return to the "good old days." The future appears bleak.

Solutions are not easy. Answers are not readily available.

We have read or heard about the Great Depression of the 1930s. Many alive today have experienced it first hand. We have witnessed exponential rates of economic growth as well as the cycle of ups and downs in our economy since World War II. We have been in a stagnant economy since 1980. Depending on our individual financial status and situation, we feel the impact of the economy in different ways and in varying degrees. Most people are content to leave economics to the economists, unless of course their immediate situations are affected. Most Christians and well-meaning church people are no exception to that general rule. It is a curious fact that Christian (religious) education has seldom addressed critically the economic activity which is basic and lies at the very core of human life. The Christian church has not provided significant leadership to assist in understanding the economic system which has control over the very well-being of its membership and of the human family. It is our hope that this study book, primarily intended for use in church schools for adults but useable in small discussion groups and by individual readers, will meet a need by enabling the curious and the concerned to take a critical analytical peep into the contemporary U.S. economy and its impact on the lives of people and the society in general. This study makes an attempt to learn about the economic system which sustains us and which is basic to our existence in the finite material world. Its focus is the U.S. economy. It is not a textbook on economics although the very nature of the subject dealt with draws it into subject areas normally found in textbooks on economics. It does not talk about stock market or profitable investments or how to manage your money. It offers an analysis (what is) of contemporary U.S. economy with the intention and hope that after reading each topic the readers will reflect on it and make value judgements (what ought to be) in the light of their faith and beliefs. Our attempt is not to provide answers but to raise the right kind of questions.

*The Gospel and Money*

This study was commissioned as a part of the Goals for the 80s of the Church of the Brethren General Board with the purpose of broadening our understanding about the economy of which we are a part and to encourage us to evaluate our economic system in the light of the gospel. A question obviously arises: Why would a church want its members to get into this complex, technical, and controversial subject, which hitherto has been the domain of highly qualified economists, who, so far, have not been able to fathom its manifestations much less deal successfully with its many problems? And other questions follow: Why should American Christians study or be concerned about the economic system which overall has been good for them and has made most of them prosper over the last two hundred years?

These are legitimate questions to raise. Christians must be concerned about economic life because economic activity and discourse lie at the very heart of human experience. Because it deals with a fundamental feature of human life, economics also engages the discipline of ethics. Biblical faith is concerned with economic life. Jesus spoke to concerns related to economics more than any other single social issue. The commandments admonish us not to steal or covet, and many teachings in the Bible ask us to be concerned about economic welfare and general happiness. The ethical concept of justice is basic in all that the church stands for. Because of the crucial joining of ethics and economics, the church must concern itself with all aspects of economic life, including a critical understanding of the system which sustains that economic life as well as undergirds the institutional church. Most observers would agree that the separation of economic life from ethical criticism has contributed to vast exploitation and misery, dehumanization of culture and resulted in an inner conflict in the motives of persons.

The church in the United States needs to address economic

issues at this time particularly because it is in this realm that the challenge to ministry will likely be greatest during this decade. That is true on at least two counts: first, because basic structural changes are occurring in the economy which are likely to cause threatening experiences for everyone in the years just ahead; secondly, because church people who have normally understood God as blessing them with an ever increasing material standard of living will become increasingly disillusioned when their incomes level off or begin to decline. They will be looking for answers and the church is where they will turn for answers. There is another important reason to focus on the economy. A significant policy shift is taking place in the area of how this nation will address the problems of the poor.

As people who are trying to live the Kingdom of God on this earth, Christians must evaluate the economic system carefully because it is not working right. The injustices and inequalities it generates do not fit the concept of the Kingdom of God. Moreover, morality and ethics have always been regarded as central to the Christian life. The Christian community has always struggled with the kinds of persons Christians should be and the actions they should take. Holding the Bible as the charter document for the Christian moral life, the Christian community has sought faithful response to God in matters of daily affairs, and it has endeavored to shape life in keeping with what ought to be.

Religion has a unique function in every society and the church as a religious institution has a vital role in contemporary society. In addition to its nurturing and comforting tasks, the church has the role of a social critic. The prophetic role is one of the important contributions of the church to society. In this role the church is one institution whose task it is to raise consistently the moral question. In response to every social policy, every institutional and social configuration, the church has the right to ask "Whose interests are being served? Is justice being accomplished?"

*Ethics and Economics*

Ethics, (the science of moral life) deals with right and wrong. Economics deals with money. It would seem that they must have something to do with one another. It so happens that the relationship between the two frequently ends up with the latter preventing actions which for the former is a matter of basic duty. For example, ethics tells us that it is a duty to work; economics says full employment is highly unlikely. Ethics says that we should care for those who are unable to care for themselves; economics says that social welfare programs are inflationary. Ethics calls for equitable tax structures; economics replies that heavy taxation will result in a "flight" of capital and an erosion of a sound capital base. And one could list many more examples.

Have ethics and economics always been in an adversary relationship? It seems, at least in principle, they should agree. If ethics is the study of right conduct, then economics, which concerns itself with business and industry as a part and parcel of human conduct generally, ought to be a subdivision of ethics. That is the traditional concept—that economics is to ethics as a part is to the whole. That is the view that characterized our Judeo-Greek-Christian civilization for two hundred years, almost up to the publication of Adam Smith's *Wealth of Nations* in 1776. Moral philosophy is one of the ancestors of economics. Only gradually did economics gain autonomy as a separate branch of learning. Plato, in his ethical system, discussed but one properly economic question: the division of labor. Like Plato, Aristotle endorsed Socrates' position that "to have few wants is God-like."

The Greek outlook on the division of labor and the accumulation of wealth prevailed in European thought until the advent of medieval scholasticism. By the thirteenth century, inquiry into the satisfaction of human wants had become part of a wholistic theological system. The central tenets of early Christian ethics as applied to economic life were the existence of hierarchy and order in society, the providential origin of the individual's appointed station in life, and the obligation incumbent upon all to practice justice in the distribution of resources as well as in human relationships. Centuries later, Albert the Great, Thomas Aquinas, and Antoninus of Florence elaborated guidelines to be obeyed by merchants, craftsmen, and noblemen in setting just prices, assessing taxes, determining proper lending practices, and making right use of superfluous goods. They stressed the ancient patristic doctrine that the earth's goods had a common destination—to meet the needs of all persons.

For several centuries thereafter the biblical doctrine of stewardship continued to influence the morality of economic life in Europe. The idea of land, labor, and capital as abstract factors in a process whose overt aim was to produce wealth was incomprehensible to most people. Work and accumulation of wealth had not become proper subjects for independent analysis. The idea of the propriety of a system organized on the basis of personal gain had not yet taken root. Neither had a self-contained economic world emerged separated from its moral context.

By the 17th century, commerce had already acquired new dimensions and new legitimacy in daily practice. Industry had begun to harness mechanical inventions to tasks of production, to concentrate a labor force, to abide by the law of capital accumulation, and to adjust itself to the demands of what was becoming a competitive market. "Man" became *homo oeconomicus* and all that was needed was a doctrine to explain him.

In 1776, Adam Smith did just that. He put together a philosophy of "political economy" in a book of some one thousand pages entitled *An Inquiry into the Nature and Causes of the Wealth of Nations*. This book was, in effect, the Declaration of Independence severing economics from moral philosophy. With its publication, economics became a separate discipline. An essential difference between Christian economics and the secular school started by Adam Smith lies in their respective concept of justice. The religious view holds that the earth belongs to God and that we are commanded by God to love and serve one another and that the economy was made for men and women and not the other way around. But things have never been the same in the economic arena since Smith published *The Wealth of Nations*.

The major significance of Smith's work does not lie in its ethics but in its tendency to discuss economic questions as if economics were a natural science, thereby short-circuiting questions of right and wrong altogether. Sir Isaac Newton's method of inquiry treating things as things was perhaps more defensible than Smith's approach of treating persons as things, which they certainly are not.

The great economists after Smith—Ricardo, Mill, Malthus, Marx, Jevons, Marshall, Keynes—remained moral reformers at heart, directing their analyses toward contemporary problems. But now that economics had acquired a life of its own, neither ethics nor theology provided norms or direction. Even Marx, a passionate moral critic in the *Communist Manifesto*, remained utterly detached from considerations of morality in *Das Kapital.*

Today, economics has become both the most abstractly mathematical and the most practically applicable of all the social sciences. It has achieved great virtuosity in handling means, but it is no longer competent to evaluate ends or ideals. The preceding historial overview of the relationship of ethics and economics may help us to understand how we got where we are and to chart where we go from here.

While we are on the topic of ethics and economics, it is important to point out that the terms "morality" and "ethics" tend to be ascribed very narrow meanings by many people. For example, many believe that morality is private virtue, such as honesty and sexual decency, and that ethics is rules for right and wrong personal conduct. Some argue that morality and ethics are subjective matters which ought not to be permitted to upset the workings of economic life. Another dimension of the ethics-economics relationship worthy of mention is that when our own security, comforts, and pleasures are at stake, the temptation to rationalize is certainly very great. Christians tend to be complacent concerning the essential justice of economic institutions because Christian interpreters themselves are largely drawn from, or are dependent on, social groups that benefit most from the economy.

Christians must acknowledge that the economic order is not autonomous, that it stands under the judgment of God as known in Christ. We must broaden our understanding of morality and ethics. We must raise value-based ethical questions like these: What do we regard as good, and why do we think of it as good? Why is something better than something else, or worse? Why is one decision right and another wrong? Why is some particular thing more important and something else less so? What is the good life?

Other compelling questions for Christians as we assess economic life are: Is the economic system just and equitable? Is it moral? Does it meet the needs of *all* people? Does it take into consideration the social costs and consequences it creates, deliberately or otherwise? Does it build or disintegrate community? Does it preserve or destroy God's creation? Who controls the economy and for whose benefit?

*Causes of Suffering*

Above all else, a study of our economic system is critical for discerning ways in which it is oppressive, both domestically and internationally. As the beneficiaries of the most powerful economy ever created in the world, this discernment is a prerequisite step in our journey of liberation. Whether we like it or not, the oppression which our economic system perpetrates on those outside it places us automatically in the category of oppressors. Why is this so? Because oppression is always two-sided, with the exploiter on one side and the victim on the other. It is also the nature of oppression that it destroys humanity on both sides although in different ways: on the one side through evil (sin), on the other side through suffering. The suffering of the oppressed is the sin of the oppressors.

The two sidedness of oppression makes it mandatory that the process of liberation begin simultaneously on both sides. The problem, however, is that while the oppressed of the Third World have been developing their own theology of liberation (based mainly on their economic sufferings), Christians of the Northern Hemisphere have not addressed seriously their own situation of affluence. It is easy for us to acknowledge the need of others for liberation, but we are unwilling to recognize ourselves as their oppressors. A critical look at our economic system may give us insights necessary to work on both sides of oppression in reaching toward the goal of the new and open community of humanity in which there are no longer either oppressors or oppressed.

A primary goal of this study is to broaden the understanding of church people about the U.S. economic system, capitalism, and to assist them in critiquing it from a faith perspective. Therefore, the study attempts to be both analytical and factual in order to enable readers to obtain a comprehensive view of the economy as well as to see how its various components fit together. It also deals with some of the major problem areas in the economy. However, it does not attempt to provide definitive solutions to the many questions it may raise.

The study has been organized into 13 chapters authored by four persons. Chapter 2 and Chapter 5 are written by T. Wayne Rieman, a retired Professor of Religion, Manchester College, North Manchester, Indiana. Chapter 3 is authored by Murray Wagner, Jr., Professor of Church History at the Bethany Biblical Seminary, Oak Brook, Illinois. The dialogue on global economy in Chapter 12 is between Robert Scott, an Anglican priest from New Zealand who is currently the Secretary on Racism with the New Zealand Council of Churches, and Shantilal Bhagat. The rest of the chapters are written by Shantilal Bhagat, who is on the national staff of the Church of the Brethren General Board, Elgin, Illinois, serving as their United Nations representative and consultant on global justice issues.

The study has been divided into thirteen chapters so it can be used in a thirteen session church school quarter. The content may appear overwhelming for a 45-minute session, but prior reading and advance preparation should enable participants to have a profitable educational experience together. The Leader's Guide will assist leaders to focus the attention of the class on key issues for each session.

# 2
# Biblical Perspective

Perspective refers to seeing something in relation to something else. A biblical perspective pertains to special ways of viewing that are in accord with the revelation that comes from the Bible. The Bible has unique stories, values, traditions, and ways of looking at life.

The Bible is not a textbook on economics. It has many things to tell us about spiritual matters, but it also is concerned about material things. The Bible has thousands of references to economic matters: wealth and poverty, luxury and deprivation, honest work and exploitation, labor and wages, borrowing and lending, use and misuse of land, interest rates, the pride and perils of possessions, and the kindred sins of greed and covetousness are dealt with directly or inferentially on hundreds of pages of both Old and New Testaments. In terms of the number of verses, the subject of wealth and poverty is the second most dominant motif in the Bible. One out of every ten verses in the synoptic gospels is about the rich and the poor. In Luke, it is one out of every seven verses. One out of five verses in James deals in some way about money, possessions, the rich, and the poor.

Jesus was not an economist. How much he studied the economic system of his day is not clear. What is clear is that he knew the consequences of the system. He was keenly aware of wealth and poverty, the attitudes which caused them, the deprivation of the poor, and the spiritual consequences

accruing to those whose trust was in material things (Matt.
6:24ff). Jesus "knew what was in man" (John 2:25), lusts and
cravings for more. Who can forget the stories of the rich
farmer (Luke 12:16-20) and the rich young ruler (Mark
10:17-22)?

There is no one biblical perspective on economics. Diversity prevails. Let's take a quick historical survey of Old Testament and New Testament perspectives on economic matters.

*Economic Concern in the Old Testament*

Among the nomad herdsmen of Genesis, wealth was
measured primarily in terms of the size of flocks. Fertility of
the womb, large flocks, and many children indicated God's
blessing (Gen. 12:1-8; 15:1-21; 13:15-16).

In the later agrarian society of Canaan, wealth was
measured in terms of possession of land. Land speculation
emerged and inequities developed. Some of the poor sank to
the bottom of the social ladder. Slavery was practiced.

Humanitarian laws were promulgated to protect the poor
from oppression and exploitation. Much of the Covenant Code
of Exodus (20:22 to 23:33) was concerned with economic inequities. These scriptures sought even distribution of land and
wealth. Money was to be lent without interest. Slaves were to
be freed after a time of servitude. Bribes were forbidden. The
poor were given access to the resources of the land.

After the institution of the monarchy in Israel (ca. 1000
B.C.), a social change occurred that widened the gap between
the rich and the poor. The modest household of Saul was expanded rapidly by David, while the magnificent court of
Solomon radiated pomp and splendor. Seemingly, according to
the perspective of the writer of Chronicles, this had the blessing of God. Both riches and honor come from God (1 Chron.
29:12).

The prophets of the 7th and 8th centuries (B.C.), however,
had another view of economics. The prophets saw that the

splendor of the court and temple was at the expense of their
fellow citizens who lived in squalor (Isa. 1:11-17; Micah 3:9-12).
God required economic justice! This is the unending cry of
Isaiah, Amos, Hosea, and Micah.

Amos' castigation of the wealthy was blistering! They
lived in the lap of luxury, ate expensive foods, drank wine from
huge bowls, enjoyed summer and winter homes, and slept on
ivory beds and couches (Amos 3:15; 6:18). God despised the ill-
gotten wealth. The prophets were unequivocal. God was
against the wealthy. It is not that Amos denounced possessions themselves, but he saw wealth as always aquired at the
expense of the powerless poor. Acquisition of power and
wealth was achieved by trampling over the heads of the poor
(2:7; 4:1; 5:11; 8:4). God is always on the side of the poor. God
was a God of justice (5:24), who willed economic fair play. Such
justice involved a more even distribution of land and wealth
(Micah 2:2; 4:3-4; 3:2-3). Micah was a radical economic
reformer! The land reforms of Latin America and Asia in our
era partake of this prophetic justice.

At a later time in the life of Israel other radical social and
economic reforms were instituted. The Deuteronomic Code
(Deut. 12—26) reflects these reforms. Justice in the courts on
financial decisions; standardization of weights, measures,
wages, and interest rates; protection of privacy; systematic
distribution of food to the poor; and grub stakes for released
slaves were at the heart of this radical reform.

The Holiness Code (Lev. 17-26), proposed at about the time
of the fall of Jerusalem, contained a number of humanitarian
laws. Included among them were proposals to protect the poor,
the commandment to love the neighbor as oneself, and the pro-
posal for the year of jubilee every fifty years which would
restore land to the original owners, thus maintaining the small
farm.

During the Hellenistic period (after 322 B.C.), there was
considerable social and political unrest. It created unfortunate

economic conditions which forced many Jews into deprivation and despair. The idea of poverty as an ideal emerged among some groups. Sects appeared who proudly accepted poverty as a special mark of piety. The Essenes of Qumran referred to themselves as "The Poor." The theology of poverty looked to God for deliverance. Poverty was passively accepted, believing that divine deliverance came in the end.

Another perspective on economic matters persisted through most of Israel's history. It existed in Jesus' day, and it is very much alive among the affluent of our era. This view held that economic prosperity was a sign of virtue and God's approval (Ps. 1:1-3 and 112; Prov. 15:6, 21:20). Poverty was divine punishment for moral failures (Prov. 21:17).The book of Job protests this view vigorously, and maintains that physical and economic conditions are not adequate tests of divine approval.

In five brief statements, Peter Davids (*Sojourners,* February 1978) summarizes Old Testament perspectives on economics with special reference to lifestyles.

1. The Old Testament does not value asceticism for its own sake, but rather looks toward the collective well-being of the people of God as the ideal.

2. Since collective prosperity is the ideal and since all property belongs to God, the Law contains regulations tending to minimize capital accumulation and actualize relative social equality.

3. God presents himself . . . as one who is especially on the side of the poor.

4. A mark of the true people of God is that they identify with God's interest in the poor and copy God's action in relieving them. Therefore, a life of relative ease in the midst of the suffering of others is never seen as good.

5.  The Old Testament views trust in and commitment to God,
    irrespective of the consequences of this action, as the deter-
    mining factor in the pious person's lifestyle.

*New Testament Teachings on Economic Themes*
    The recurring themes of the New Testament are sin and
the good news of salvation. Nowhere does it discuss an
economic system as such. The New Testament, however, also
addresses itself to the consequences of economic matters:
crushing poverty, exploitation of the poor by the rich, perils of
prosperity, callousness of the rich, twin evils of greed and
covetousness, folly of worrying about material goods, tran-
sitoriness of wealth and possessions, and other related issues.
    The New Testament also has specific teachings on
economic themes. *The earth and its bountiful resources are
good.* There is a legitimate place for the physical world,
material things, and fleshly hungers and thirsts. Materiality is
not decried in either Old or New Testaments. Creation is good.
*Christianity may be the most materialistic of all religions.* So it
is asserted. It is true in the sense that Jesus and the early
church gave great attention to matters of wealth and poverty
and the proper handling of possessions.
    *We are responsible for the economic welfare of others.* The
New Testament teaches this in language and story that cannot
be mistaken. If we have this world's goods and we see those in
need and if we close our heart to them, we do not have God's
love in us (1 John 3:17).
    Jesus states our responsibility in unmistakable words. He
told the good Samaritan story. It teaches us that neighbor love
ought to reach all needy persons (Luke 10:30-37). We know
that half the world's people live in relative poverty, about a
billion people are malnourished, and a half billion are starving.
We pay so little attention to the economic arrangements that
condemn them to such poverty.
    In the great judgment story (Matt. 25), the provision of

food, clothing, and shelter and the visitation of the sick are absolutely central. Those who show no concern for the economic well-being of the poor and of strangers face a dismal future. Jesus' language is powerful.

*The kingdom of God, Jesus' central concern, is not a material kingdom.* It does not involve geographic boundaries, armies, taxes, or possessions. It is the realm of God's activity; it is here and now and it is to come more fully. Spiritual as it is, Jesus' descriptive parables of it use economic categories frequently. Note these terms: seeds and sowing, good and bad soils, wheat and tares, buying and selling, merchants and pearls of great price, taxes and tribute money, wealth and poverty, feasting and fasting, fields and vineyards, talents and investments, fruitful and barren trees, wise providers for the future and the foolishly irresponsible, and fish and sheep and bushel baskets. The kingdom pervades the economic world, or shall we say that economics invades the kingdom?

Jesus was well aware of numerous schemes in Israel to effect land reform, to redistribute wealth, and to avoid exploitation of the poor. His early manifesto (Luke 4:16-21) indicates his identification with such concerns. He sought drastic changes. While others accepted the monarchy, the temple, and the priesthood as valid and permanent institutions, he supported none of these. Jesus saw temple practices as economically exploitive and religiously pervertive (Matt. 12:6; Luke 20:46—21:6). Jesus spent many of his energies bucking the systems of his day.

John Howard Yoder argues convincingly that Jesus proposed economic restructuring (*The Politics of Jesus*, Eerdmans, pp. 34-41). His proclamation of good news for the poor, of release to captives, and of freeing the oppressed was not simply rhetoric! Society was to be changed! He announced a new regime, a visible socio-political economic restructuring. Clearly he harked back to the jubilee year (Lev. 25), in which land was to be redistributed, debts annulled, and slaves released. He proposed costly, far reaching economic acts, system changing. Anyone who reduces Jesus to mere rhetoric and private ethics misses the radical dimensions of his actions. See Luke 6:24-25, 30-36. A new age of economic realism had begun!

*Our Thinking Is Full of Errors*
The pagan world in which we live foists erroneous thinking upon us. It would deny many teachings of the Bible.

*Life consists in the abundance of things. Life is better if we have more acres, more tractors, more shop machinery, more gadgets in the household, more cars and clothes and money in the bank.* The love of luxury, the lust for an ever-increasing standard of living, and for climbing the economic ladder of upward mobility are incongruous with the life of the kingdom. Kingdom living turns things around. Jesus, the chief revealor of the kingdom, showed us downward mobility. He washed feet. He was a servant. His life was the richest we have ever seen, yet he owned nothing.

*What we do with our substance affects only ourselves.* "It's mine, I can do with it as I please." So the pagan world tells us. Many of us believe it. We live that way. We farm our fields, spend our substance, expend our energies, just as if we were the owners of all that we possess.

At the heart of the Hebrew-Christian heritage is the recognition that we own nothing. "The earth is the Lord's and the fullness thereof" (Ps. 24:1). "We brought nothing into the world, and we cannot take anything out of the world" (1 Tim. 6:7). We are stewards, not owners. We are entrusted with talents, energies, money, and properties for a season. But only for a season. Every day is an accounting time.

*Material blessings are an assurance of God's blessing.* Although this idea can be found in certain portions of the Old Testament, the prophets objected to it. The book of Job argues against this position. There is no indication that Jesus supported it. Rather, it is hard for the rich to enter the Kingdom (Luke 18:24).

*Money, land, and other possessions are evil.* Our pagan world does not tell us this. No! Our consumptive society tells us the opposite. There are some good people, however, who think the material world is evil. The biblical perspective does not support this. It holds that creation is good and that the earth is the Lord's. Jesus seemingly lived with few possessions. He did not tell us that money is evil, though it is difficult to control. What Jesus did expect was that his disciples would make a break with possessions so that they could serve one master and seek the Kingdom first (Matt. 6:19, 21, 24, 33).

### The Hazards of Economics

Why is the Bible preoccupied with economic issues? These concerns are found in wisdom literature, in prophetic writings, throughout the Gospels, and elsewhere in the New Testament. Why this preoccupation? Because the hazards are great.

Jesus and others give warnings in stern language about money and properties. Possessions are perilous because they so easily separate person from person, and persons from God. They so easily possess their possessors.

So easily we are "rich in things and poor in soul." So easily we get into predicaments like the rich young ruler (Luke 18:18-23). We are attracted to Jesus. We listen to his call to discipleship, and we look at our possessions. We weigh the two things in our minds. Then, like the young man, we turn away. Money talks! This is the ultimate peril of possessions. Not only is it hard for the rich to enter the kingdom of God. It is also difficult for those who are trying to be rich to enter the Kingdom. Apostle Paul told young Timothy that "the love of money is the root of all evils" (1 Tim. 6:10).

The Bible is concerned with economic issues because economic affairs are inextricably related to kingdom living. There are those who would separate the work-a-day world of buying and selling, owning and producing, managing and accumulating from the spiritual life. But it can't be done! We are whole beings. What we do with the work of our hands and mind, the way we handle land and other possessions, is inevitably related to our inner lives. "Where your treasure is, there will your heart be also" (Matt. 6:21).

There is a constant danger that we will put money and material things first and God second. We live in a culture that puts profits above people's interests, that refuses to control profits despite what ruthless profit making does to powerless people near or far away.

Money is not evil (1 Tim. 6:10). We need not feel guilty about possessing it if we share it generously and acquire it honestly. Jesus did not teach mindless faith. He did not denounce thinking about clothing for the children, or tools for field and factory, or housing against rain and cold, or food for the family. Matthew 6:34 is properly translated: "Don't *worry* about tomorrow." It is possible to manage our financial affairs so that they do not dominate our minds.

Economic affairs and our standard of living are not merely private matters. They are critical in our discipleship. Money and possessions are central issues in human experience. Our use of them reveals more about ourselves than almost anything else. For Jesus, the use of money was a deeply spiritual issue that was closely tied to the central core of individuals.

Finally, the Bible is preoccupied with economic issues because of who we are and what we are as humans. It is good to be human. We are made in God's image—that's the most wonderful thing about us as humans. We are made for fellowship, comradeship, and communion with God and other humans. Like a key and a lock are made for each other, so we were made for God.

We are people with hungers and thirsts. They are good. Saint Augustine affirms that our hearts are restless until they rest in God. Unfortunately, often we seek to satisfy our deepest hungers by grasping for things, for money, and for possessions.

The biblical writers were realists. Like Jesus, they "knew what was in man." They knew the glory of the created world and also the dangers into which we can fall as we deal with its rich resources. Human capacities to pervert, pollute, and misuse the resources of the good earth are nearly unlimited. Because of this, Jesus and the prophets were highly sensitive to the poor, to the dangers of accumulating wealth, and to the subtle perils of possessions.

Life does not consist in the abundance of things. Eternal life does not lie in wealth or what it buys. We need bread, but we cannot live by bread alone. Things do not satisfy the hungers of the heart.

# 3
# The Church and
# Economics through
# History

Neither the Bible nor the early church gives either a constitutional draft of an ideal political order or a classic statement on Christian economic theory. Those who go prooftexting in search of biblical prescriptions on economic and political organization will inevitably find the chapter and verse to support their prior convictions. The Scriptures attest to a variety of beliefs and practices already evident during the ancient period of church history. While virtually every Christian tradition, institution, and theory makes its appeal to the authority of the early church, in actual fact there was a plurality of religious confessions and social attitudes in primitive Christianity.

Though the church's history from the biblical period through the first three centuries was diverse in economic attitudes, there were prevailing concerns about riches, property, and the distribution of goods. Early Christians commonly demanded a detachment from property, voiced a radical critique of luxury possessions, and sought to break the material barriers between the rich and the poor within Christian communities.

One of the most vivid and often cited expressions of early Christian attempts to resolve the destructive economic tensions between rich and poor is found in the Acts of the Apostles.

All who believed were together and had all things in common;

and they sold their possessions and goods and distributed them
to all, as any had need. . . . No one said that any of the things
which he possessed was his own, but they had everything in common. . . . There was not a needy person among them, for as many
as were possessors of lands or houses sold them, and brought the
proceeds of what was sold and laid it at the apostles' feet; and
distribution was made to each as any had need (Acts 2:44, 45;
4:34, 35).

The community of common goods described in the Acts account was conditioned by the expectation that the end of the
world was near. A further consideration was the community's
lack of institutional organization. There was a spontaneous
and voluntary character to this early form of "love communism." The impulse was inspired by the spirit of *koinonia*,
not the requirements of organization. The measures taken to
hold possessions in common were intended to make both grinding poverty and inordinate riches impossible.

As eschatological hopes abated, the spontaneity faded. Attitudes toward possessions began to accommodate to the
social norms of the Roman Empire. Care of the poor was done
by church officers who collected alms from wealthier members
and distributed aid to Christians living in poverty.

As Christianity spread, the social status of new converts
began to affect the economic theory and practice of the church.
Most of Christianity's early recruits were not from the lowest
economic strata; that is, it was not a slave religion. The majority came from the ranks of laborers, craftsmen, and small
businessmen. People from these economic ranks had a high
estimate of the value of manual labor. Early Christians were
industrious and frugal people who supported each other in love
and, at the same time, expected just compensation for honest
labor. Consequently, the labors of the middle classes of early
Christianity led to the acquisition of modest amounts of property, whether or not it was sought deliberately.

By the time of the third-century persecutions, church membership often included converts from the upper strata. Even if the majority of Christians came from simple origins, numbers from the ranks of the high born and wealthy increased. Once this happened, the mission of the church had to address all social classes. Otherwise it would have closed its ranks in segregated communities of ascetic discipline. The direction in favor of social universalism left the theology of the poor and the consequent critique of property to a minority of dissenters within the total Christian community. By the time Christianity became official in Constantine's fourth-century decrees, the economic attitudes of the Christian majority had already moderated to narrow the difference between church and society.

There is, nonetheless, a clear witness from the earliest tradition that stands in judgment against modern consumerism and extravagant wealth in the midst of poverty and economic oppression. In the biblical recognition of what the earliest theologians called original sin, the primitive church understood the crisis of property to be the crisis of the human condition. It is the crisis created by human pride; pride in pursuit of power and wealth at the expense of the poor and afflicted, be they the slaves of first-century Rome, or the starving populations of the twentieth-century Third World.

## The Medieval Church

The Constantinian grant of monopoly privileges to the church endowed a once persecuted sect with the authority to discipline the whole body politic in spirit and in flesh. By political force, that holy alliance between the pope and the emperor regulated all activity by a set of theological absolutes. In theory, all secular authority flowed from God through his agent on earth, the Catholic church. A fundamental characteristic of medieval society's theocentric world view was that its historical sense was static. The notion of dynamic social change in the hope for progress, a given in modern economic theories of growth and expansion, was not a supposition that guided the thought of church theologians in their treatises on the social order. The purpose of life was not "to get ahead" or to accumulate wealth and property, but to obey God's will according to the instruction of the church.

Medieval society, a cultural tradition that held sway for more than a thousand years, did not look upon the making of money either as a sign of God's favor or as a noble achievement. It was rather seen as a form of antisocial behavior and thus a sin against the divine order. Church authorities argued that commercial pursuits were corrupting to the soul. Lending money at interest was forbidden; therefore, banking was considered an immoral activity. The market system that determines the price of goods and services by whatever the consumer will bear was unthinkable. Prices were fixed and regulated by guilds and by governments according to a standard considered to be just by the church. Sociologist R. H. Tawney observed that before the advent of expansionary economic theories, people called avarice and greed by their right names. They "had not learned to persuade themselves that greed was enterprise and avarice economy."

However, and here the however is writ very large, the economic facts of the medieval society were harsh and oppressive. They represented a brute reality that contradicts the nostalgia of modern-day critics of technical society who yearn for the peasant community. Some people lament for a past age when all things were held by a symmetry of coherence and unanimity.

Medieval society was indeed coherent. It was also unanimous. Its symmetries were those of a total society. Unanimity and coherence were enforced by Christian totalitarianism. The harmony of the order was in the covenant between the church and the institutions of feudalism. The result was an economic system that allowed a handful of nobility to live a life of luxury. It also allowed the church and its clergy to confiscate vast amounts of wealth and property for its own aggrandizement. Such was the glory of the medieval world that has disappeared, to the great consternation of those who try to pose it as an alternative to modern technological society.

What of those who were stirred to protest the wealth of the clergy and the economic abuses heaped upon the peasantry by the nobility? For centuries the medieval church showed a remarkable capacity to channel the pursuit of holiness through its monastic orders. Objectors to the wealth of the theocratic establishment were given opportunity to cultivate lives of austerity and simplicity appropriate to their understanding of the Scriptures in monastic communities that gathered within the legitimate Catholic society.

The Protestant Reformation altered the theocentric world view that had dominated the West since Constantine's official merger of church and society. The Reformation, treated below in three segments, irreversibly changed the direction of Christianity and its cultural traditions.

*Lutheranism*

Martin Luther's 1517 posting of his theses at Wittenberg rent the garments of the medieval church's total society. Luther's reformation was religious in character. He rejected the church's sacramental system of prescribing good works to penitent believers for the remission of sins. Beneath that rejection was his own agonizing struggle over the very personal question, "What must I do to be saved?" Luther left undisturbed the political and economic assumptions of the society and remained medieval in his defense of the divine rights of its authorities. Nonetheless, his theological challenge to the church's claim to be the exclusive interpreter of God's will set in motion forces that have influenced the rise of modern economic and political attitudes.

For Luther, there was only one way to secure salvation, by faith alone. Only by standing alone before God in the recognition of one's total depravity could the believer hope for saving grace. If salvation depended only on individual faith, unmediated by clergy or regulated by sacraments, then the controlling authority of the church was undermined. The individual conscience was allowed to interpret the will of God through the study of Scripture. It was this Lutheran teaching that unwittingly struck at the heart of the medieval society. As individuals were instructed to obey their religious conscience, they made corporate social interests more important than theological obligations that required conformity. Such was Luther's inadvertent stimulus to the rise of sovereign individualism so basic to modern economic competition.

## Calvinism

Thirty years after Luther's first protest at Wittenberg, John Calvin gave Protestantism the rigorous character of a new age of intense puritans. They formed austere ranks of achievers in pursuit of the kingdom of God through self-denial and hard work. Calvin knew not that his *Institutes of the Christian Religion* would become the marching orders for a race of stalwarts who are now claimed as pioneering heroes by the modern age of economic enterprise and expansionary progress.

How did Calvin's intimidating theology of double predestination become one of the motivating factors in the rise of capitalism? Calvin reasoned that God is in no way influenced by what each person does in this world. Since God arbitrarily chooses to save some people but not all, then salvation must, in fact, be predetermined.

Of course, the big question for the terrified believer is how one can know if one is among the elect. Calvin argued that no one can really ever know. Only God knows who will be saved and who will be damned. Since the world and everything in it has been organized to serve the glory of God, those who have been saved are literally programmed from the foundations of the universe to fulfill the divine commandments. The elect can do no other than God's will, simply because God wills it. Moreover, everyone has an obligation to believe they are chosen. That belief must be constantly reaffirmed through unceasing activity in the performance of God's will. The evidence given in the results of faithful labor, seen concretely in the production of goods and services, is not only a kind of partial proof of election but, according to sociologist Max Weber, a necessary cause in the development of capitalist enterprise.

Calvin intended no industrial revolution. He would be highly critical of the materialism and the consumerism of technological societies that have developed out of the compulsion to produce. Yet his deterministic theology has become, by default if not by design, one of the most deeply imbedded characteristics of societies that invest their hopes for economic progress in GNP growth and expansionary enterprise. The behavior of those Protestant asectics, who denied themselves as much of earthly pleasure as any monk and approached their labor with as much a sense of calling as any member of the clergy, is still the driving force of secular capitalism, long after the religious backgrounds have been forgotten.

Calvinists always produced and accumulated more than their austere sensibilities would ever permit them to consume. Therefore they took the balance and either gave it to charity or reinvested it for industrial expansion. The Calvinists' secular descendents are those who labor, from the corporate head, to the pig farmer, to the assembly line worker. They find meaning in life through self-denial and hard work. Ask any one why they are so ordered, so efficient, so punctual: why they never eat out, take vacations, or buy a second suit. They will say they don't know, but they wouldn't know how to do it any other way.

*Anabaptism*

The "Believers' Church" types, including the sectarians of either Pietist or Anabaptist traditions, make an assumption regarding the basis of church membership that sharply distinguishes them from Calvinist polity. According to Calvin, the members of the true church were elected to the kingdom of God on or before their birth. On the contrary, Believers' Churches gather the faithful from among those who have made a free, adult choice for church membership. They have not been compelled into the fold by the force of divine determinism. Nevertheless, these sectarian traditions have also cherished the virtues of asceticism, frugality, and honest labor as a divine calling. Thus their ethical disciplines have had an immense importance on the rise of capitalist economics.

The sectarian communities would have nothing to do with the political powers and their machinations, but they did penetrate the secular order in response to God's call to "work for the night is coming." These "married monks" followed their ethic of self-denial and hard work in separatist communities. They were so conscientious in their effort to do good that as a consequence they ended up doing very well. They viewed the accumulated wealth that resulted from the productivity of the faithful as bad only insofar as it represented a temptation to idleness and sinful indulgence in the pleasures of the flesh. Wealth is not to be consumed in frivolity and gluttony, but to be distributed to all of God's children after the example of the early church's care of the poor. Or, it is to be applied toward making the earth even more productive. The sectarians, like Calvin, would be totally scandalized by the malignant Mammonism of twentieth-century technocracies that squander their treasure in waste, in luxury, and in the riotous living of consumer goods and military spending. Those are precisely the secular evils that convinced the sectarians that the true church had nothing in common with the world of political powers and industrial giants.

### A Critical Moment

The age of unlimited material growth and political expansion is of necessity about to give way to an age of scarcity and great economic disruption. The modern world of science and technology that has produced for the West massive amounts of wealth in material goods at the expense of the world's majority populations is predicated on the assumption that the earth's resources are unlimited. Behind this secular vision of the good life is a religious understanding that comes from God's very first commandment to humankind. In the beginning, God says to Adam, "Have dominion over the fish of the sea and over the birds of the air and over every living thing that moves upon the earth." That text has been used first by Christians and now by secular societies to justify unrestrained pillage and exploitation of the natural world.

Now, the unrenewable resources are diminishing down dry holes and polluted oceans. The guiding religious vision must shift the understanding of dominion from humankind as exploiter to humankind as steward, protector, and conservator of creation. The alternative is that Christianity will retrench itself into the old pieties which understood dominion as a divine right to subdue the earth for selfish material and political benefit. A new form of Christian totalitarianism will arise. The faith and the society are at a critical moment in human history. The way we choose to interpret the faith is not less than a matter of life and death.

# 4
# Brethrenomics

There are strong indications that the simple, frugal, austere lifestyle is on the wane. For all practical purposes, the American culture dominates the lives and prescribes the economic ethic for most Brethren, who seem to accept it without seriously questioning, much less challenging it.

Brethren historian Floyd E. Mallott wrote "The Dunker elder bought an automobile and stepped on the gas; out of the window went his broadbrim, followed by his wife's bonnet, followed by his whiskers." These were followed by the remainder of the distinctive attire, then many of the peculiar practices, and finally the nonresistant peace testimony.

The Church of the Brethren came to Pennsylvania from an old, feudal, stratified European society in the early part of the eighteenth century. Most of those who emigrated were poor laborers, peasants, or artisans, persecuted for their religious beliefs, living in an environment which held an unpromising economic future in their homeland. Those of the sect who had plenty shared with the many who were poor. In 1719 when Alexander Mack, the sect's leader, ran out of his own funds, the Dutch Collegiants (a Anabaptist group from Holland) donated 8,000 guilders to help the "needy Schwarzenuers."

Recognizing the poverty of the members, seeing little economic future in the area, and sensing the possibility of economic sanctions through a refusal to continue woodcutting permits in the Schwarzenau forests, Mack moved to

Surhuisterveen in northwestern Holland with forty families in May 1720. The economic situation was not very bright in the new location either. The income was low and there were periods of real hunger. Some Brethren were on relief. Again, help came from the Dutch Collegiants.

The congregation spent nine years in Holland. During the last four years they endured great economic anxiety before thirty families, including Mack's own, decided to emigrate to America. They had received glowing reports from Peter Becker and twenty other families from the Krefeld congregation who had settled in Pennsylvania in 1719.

*Brethren in a New World*

In America the Brethren faced the potential dangers of the accumulation of wealth rather than economic uncertainty or starvation. Money was able to buy more. The land was plentiful and the price was low. These factors presented a primary condition of prosperity for these poor agricultural peasants from Europe. In Pennsylvania, Brethren could own as much land as they wanted, build houses, be self-employed, develop their own farms, and accumulate wealth. This was an entirely new experience for them.

Ingrained in their European background were the values of hard work and a suspicion of idleness. Frugality and self-reliance were a part of their cultural heritage, which helped in strengthening their economic base in this new land. The desire to achieve economic security and independence were only natural. Very quickly, economic independence became the ideal among the Brethren. The church in America moved in a direction quite different from the sharing of life and property that Mack had originally envisioned. The newly adopted lifestyle of the Brethren generally absorbed the prevailing spirit of individualism.

While economic self-reliance was the norm, mutual aid played a very important role among the Brethren for a long time. Help was extended to the needy as a matter of practicing one's faith in God. On the economic level, the concept of the priesthood of all believers meant that the needs of all believers had to be met. Material questions were important along with the spiritual. Not only that, but mutuality expressed through economic sharing implied that financial matters were not altogether outside the scrutiny of the covenant community. In other words, a breech of an economic contract or a lapse in economic relationship was subject to communal disciplinary action for the restoration of wholeness.

The early Brethren lived in close community but did not espouse voluntary poverty or community of goods. Their brotherhood type of Anabaptism interpreted the principle of separation from the world less literally than either the revolutionary type (compulsory pooling of property or enforced communism) or the Hutterite type (voluntary pooling of property or Christian communism). Private property and wealth were accepted as good if used for Christian purposes rather than for personal pleasure.

*Western Migration*

The westward migration of the Brethren in the late eighteenth and throughout the nineteenth centuries is generally attributed to the persecution they received during the Revolutionary War. However, it also was the result of the dissatisfaction with one's status in the present location and reports of good cheap land ahead. During the first one hundred and fifty years in America, the Brethren spread all over the country, seeking out the best farm land for their homes and setting up farming operations. They were almost entirely rural, predominantly farmers accustomed to an agricultural economy. They were thrifty, frugal, hard-working people who were good stewards of the land. They earned a reputation for developing fine-looking farms and substantial buildings.

Simplicity of life, characteristically Brethren, led to an

insistence upon simple clothing and austere living. Practically every year between 1778 and 1909, the actions of the Annual Meeting referred in one way or another to the decisions laid down by that body against worldly possessions and ornaments and the temptations contained therein. According to Donald F. Durnbaugh, "Many of the minutes of the Annual Meetings of the nineteenth century read like a catalog of prohibitions. Among things to be spurned were bells, carpets, life insurance, lightning rods, likenesses, liquor, musical instruments, salaried ministers, secret societies, shows and fairs, tobacco, and flowered wallpaper. Although such prohibitions may be easily satirized, they represent an attempt to live simply and decently as good stewards of material resources."

*The Era of Change*

The period from 1851 is important not only because of the onset of industrialization in America but also because of the launching of the *Gospel Visitor*, a monthly journal which once again tied the Brethren together.

Many noteworthy changes took place in this period: a phenomenal rise of Brethren educational institutions (some of which were business ventures which made a profit while providing good education), the approval of Sunday schools for religious education, the establishment of foreign missions, and a more elaborate church organization with the establishment of districts and the beginning of a permanent headquarters organization which expanded as program expanded. These developments were related to the economic prosperity of the Brethren in the new land.

It was mainly under the effect of industrialization and urbanization after 1905 that the Brethren introduced the professional ministry with a formal training. The salaried pastor became the norm and the free ministry declined gradually. Economic prosperity affected the Brethren as much as any other group, and they went through a remarkable degree of social change. In the process the church moved from a stance of aloof nonconformity to a high degree of cultural conformity. It moved from a sect to becoming a denomination.

The changes which this period (1851 onward) brought to the church also produced serious tensions and a division within the denomination.

*Advice of Annual Meeting*

From their beginings the Brethren were consciously and intentionally in conflict with the larger culture surrounding them. But in America they experienced a minimum of persecution for nonconformity, and it was relatively easy for the larger culture to make inroads among them. One can see, during this period in Brethren history, how their natural suspicion of certain contemporary economic practices caused them to seek the counsel of the Annual Meeting again and again as these practices made greater inroads. It is instructive to examine the Annual Meetings' rulings on some of these practices.

*Interest-taking.* "It is considered that no member should take interest on money" (1783). "We think it is not consistent with the Gospel to take more than lawful interest" (1862).

*Investments.* "We advise the brethren not to invest their money in bank stock at all, and would advise them to be cautious of all incorporated companies" (1860). The reason given for this advice was that "persons dealing with such companies may be liable to be deceived."

Commercial procedures such as the use of notes and mortgages were permissible between members. Members could also secure patents on inventions provided the local congregation gave its consent. In 1864 the Brethren said, "The Gospel does not forbid Brethren to act as executors or administrators."

*Commercial activity.* In 1832 the Annual Meeting agreed that a brother might be a storekeeper "in cases of necessity, a brother has no other way to make a living." Twenty years later the Brethren were advised not to sell their farms and "go in for store-keeping" especially if they were ministers.

The position of the Brethren down to the end of the nineteenth century is well summarized by the Annual Meeting statement, "We would admonish the Brethren to be very careful in engaging in all kinds of business, and especially in business done by incorporated bodies, such as railroads and borrowing companies, since, by so doing, they may be brought into dangerous association with ungodly men."

*Property insurance.* Insurance became one of the key institutions of the modern industrial economy. Concern about insurance first came to Annual Meeting in 1847. Should the Brethren insure property?

A rather flexible policy was adopted that year and the decision said, "We cannot advise brethren to do so, neither could we forbid its being done, in a mutual way." Although the question was debated eight more times between 1848 and 1879, property insurance was always cautiously approved.

*Life insurance.* For the Brethren the most difficult economic question of the nineteenth century centered around the institution of life insurance. The earliest discussion took place in 1864 when the Brethren were advised "to make use of no such privilege." The next Annual Meeting explained its position in these definite words, "We do not think it right to put a money value upon human life, while we may on property." The response of the 1873 Annual Meeting to a query whether it was consistent for Brethren to have their lives insured was "It is inconsistent for brethren to do so."

By 1920 the Annual Meeting permitted taking out life insurance policies "where taking out of such policies violates no Gospel principle."

*Labor unions.* The Brethren being largely rural, no reference was made to labor unions until 1904. Membership in them was forbidden by this minute: "Labor unions as now conducted often lead to violence, and sometimes to riot and bloodshed, and as they are contrary to the spirit and teaching of the Gospel of Jesus Christ, we cannot allow our members to unite or belong to them." This position was modified in 1915: "While this Conference cannot sanction membership in any of the labor unions, yet we do not see our way clear to wholly forbid a necessary affiliation of members with labor unions, relief associations and beneficiary associations when by so doing they violate no Gospel principle."

As the industrial culture became more prevalent and the urban population increased, the place of collective bargaining was recognized, particularly after the depression of 1933. Still, the Brethren have been slow to sympathize with the labor movement. Kermit Eby, a prominent Brethren leader in the American labor movement, was generally ignored among the Brethren. Discussion on the floor of the Annual Conference in the last decade clearly indicated that the Brethren sentiments are still strong against the unionization of farm workers.

*Into the Twentieth Century*

By the time of World War I, no important aspect of business life was out of bounds for Brethren participation. The frontier period had come to an end. The movement of people from farms to cities in order to secure jobs in the growing industrial sector of the economy began to affect the Brethren. Farming came under pressure to change from a "way of life" to a profit-oriented mechanized occupation.

It was very threatening for the Brethren, but there was no way the church could stop the changes taking place in a rapidly moving industrial society. The church appeared to be fighting a losing battle in the period from 1851 to 1926.

Traditional Brethren ideas of separation from the world had become irrelevant for most members. Queries on economic concerns brought before Annual Meetings and the responses showed a high degree of social consciousness.

The emergence of a new consciousness with reference to the larger culture is clearly evident in the following resolution of the 1934 Annual Conference.

This age is one of crass materialism. Our industrial and commercial system rests upon the profit motive. The goods supplied or the service rendered are only incidental. The major emphasis is on the amount of cash balance regardless of what may entail upon society.

The love of money has filled papers and billboards with false advertisements; it has stimulated in men the desire to get without rendering service; it has glorified material achievement above social welfare and solidarity; it has made price fixing not a question of the worth of merchandise or service, but rather what one can get, and because of this, civilization is fast approaching demoralization and ultimate destruction.

Recovery is not a matter of clever technique, but the attainment of spiritual power. While our present capitalistic system may be a child of protestantism, it may be said with equal emphasis that communism, socialism and fascism are but reformed types of capitalism. . . . Neither of these economic-political systems will provide a panacea for our ills.

Therefore, we declare ourselves in sympathy with the idea of a Christian democracy in an attempt to bring about the kingdom of God on earth. We hold personality above profits. We seek an economic order based on needs instead of being left to blind conflicting impulses. We refrain from investing in or abetting institutions or corporations being run solely for profit and without due consideration for the common good.

This resolution was probably the first one of its kind where the Brethren expressed their views on the capitalistic economic system. It is a bold resolution which indicts the system for its weaknesses and upholds spiritual power as an antidote for its many ills.

The 1951 Annual Conference approved a "Statement of the

Church of the Brethren on Economic Problems." It is an ex-
cellent statement with general principles for action by individual members but does not speak to the Church's position
with respect to specific economic issues.

The "Justice and Nonviolence" paper approved by the
1977 Annual Conference includes a segment on economic
justice but does not go into the systemic causes responsible for
economic injustices in our world.

A significant development in the area of investment of
funds of the Church of the Brethren General Board and the
Church of the Brethren Pension Plan was the adoption of
investment guidelines in 1972. The guidelines have subsequently been revised in 1976 by the General Board and in
1981 by the Pension Board. They prescribe "do's and
don'ts" to help the administrators of funds in making investment decisions.

The basic stance in the guidelines is that the boards should
avoid purchasing stock in any corporation whose fundamental
approach is antagonistic to the principles held by the church.
Where there is no such conflict, the boards are asked to
endeavor "to influence the company through attending
shareholder meetings etc."

In accordance with the General Board guidelines, in
the spring of 1979, the Church of the Brethren witnessed by
placing a shareholder's resolution before the annual meeting
of the Union Carbide corporation. Resolutions have been
filed since then with Monsanto, Rockwell International,
General Electric, Bendix, Pillsbury, Sears, and American
Home Products. The resolutions dealt with a variety of
issues like racial justice in South Africa, nuclear weapons
activity, reduction in product advertising to children
(especially of heavily-sugared foods), "excessive and
gratuitous violence" on TV programs, and appointment of
an impartial committee to review the problems of infant for-
mula use.

*Where Is the Church Today?*

While the institutions of the church have been asked to follow investment guidelines, there is no way of knowing to what extent such guidelines are observed by individual members, congregations, and districts. It is also difficult to determine just how resolutions of the Annual Conference have affected the social conscience of individual members and congregations. Growing industrialization and urbanization have changed the picture for the Brethren just as they have for most of the rest of the people of the land. As this change has taken place, the Brethren economic ethic has begun to assimilate the basic processes and structures of the economic system which it long resisted and against which it fought in the latter half of the nineteenth century.

Floyd Mallott, who was quoted in the opening of this chapter, was much concerned about the effect of industrialization on the Brethren, whom he called "simple Sermon-on-the-Mount Christians" of peasant background. He found that some of the Brethren adaptations to the changing environment were good, but overall he was uneasy. The process of assimilation into the larger culture has gone a long way challenging what little remains of the ascetic aspect of the economic ethic of the Brethren.

# 5
# Economic Myths

Economic myths abound! It is our intention in this chapter to look at a number of prevailing economic myths. We hope to challenge them, to explore their factual bases, and to look at them from the vantage point of the Christian faith.

Myth 1. *God helps those who help themselves.*

This myth is sometimes quoted as if it had biblical authority. Really, it is a cliche used by those who have made it in economic affairs. It tends to sanction aggressive economic activity with few questions asked about methods employed. Approval is given to self-centered free enterprise. It fails to recognize that free enterprise is seldom free.

Presently, family farms are declining in number, smaller companies are becoming subsidiaries of huge conglomerates, bankruptcies occur at unprecedented rates, the corporate elite wields more and more power, and multinational corporations gobble up hundreds of millions of acres of good land and other resources. Powerful corporations and people are helping themselves to disproportionate shares of the world's wealth and privileges.

Let's not be so simple-minded as to believe that God blesses all of this! The biblical faith knows nothing of such help.

The God of the biblical faith has always been on the side of the poor. Jesus' words are caustic: "Woe to the rich."

Myth 2. *Money talks!*

What is implied by this phrase? What does money say?

Money keeps the wheels of the economy moving. It provides endless varieties of goods and services: food, clothing, shelter, education, health care, legal aid, travel, conferences, books, arts, and a thousand other useful things. It builds roads, bridges, hospitals, and schools. Money is useful. It does help to get things done. It is never evil in itself.

There's a sinister side to the phrase. It has evil innuendoes. There is a subtle insinuation that money buys people, exploits, corrupts, and perverts. And it does! The Old Testament prophets saw money corrupting judges, priests, and prophets. It made greedy people tamper with weights and balances. They saw the rich and powerful exploiting poor widows and reducing some of God's children to slavery.

Money talks today too. The rich are favored in the courts. They seldom spend time in jail. Our prisons are filled with the poor, the minorities, the powerless. Money talks!

Money sometimes tones down preachers; it quiets their voices on certain issues. Laymen and women, likewise, may stretch the truth and engage in shady practices to turn extra dollars in their direction. Money convinces many people that bigger is better, that a job with a higher salary is a better job with greater happiness.

Some even argue that everyone has their price. They think there is no one who can't be bought. Dozens of the ancient prophets could not be bought. Jesus couldn't be bought. He refused to sell his soul for self-aggrandizement, popularity, or political gain. A whole roster of the contemporary faithful can be compiled of those who couldn't be bought: Viktor Frankl, Cesar Chavez, Martin Luther King, Jr., Mother Teresa, Dorothy Day, Albert Schweitzer, and others.

Money entices, corrupts, and persuades some. But there are those who are not beguiled by it. Not everyone has a price!

Myth 3. *Poverty is inevitable.*

Jesus is misquoted frequently to bolster this myth (Mark 14:7). Well-intending people argue, "Even if the wealth of the world were redistributed equally, in a few months or years, the present inequalities would recur." It is probably true. It is a sad commentary, not on the incompetence of those who slip to the bottom of the pile, but on human greed, manipulation, and exploitation by the powerful. Why blame the victims of our society?

Poverty is the result of human decisions; it is no accident; its causes are known. Poverty is part of our economic system. It is a disorder of our economy. We permit poverty and unemployment. Productive work is impossible for millions.

Most of us participate in this economic disorder. Our privileged affluence is at the expense of the poor in our country and in the Third World.

Jesus did not act as if poverty were inevitable. His ministry was "Good News for the poor," and he hoped to bring deliverance from the bondage of poverty (Luke 4:16-21). Surely this was part of his salvation.

It is now possible to eliminate compulsory poverty. Henry Kissinger said that it could be done in a decade. Arnold Toynbee reminds us that "our generation is the first to possess the means required to eliminate poverty and hunger on a global scale. All we lack is the will." Poverty is not the will of God.

Myth 4. *Life consists in the abundance of things.*

Of course Christians do not say this. But subtly many Christians and pagan materialists have accepted the myth that life is infinitely better with more money and the things it buys. Functionally, many of us act as if it were true.

Arnold Toynbee argues that the paramount aim of the western world is economic expansion for every individual, for every social class, and for every nation. Now it has become a worldwide aim. He says that this aim has to be abandoned. It is immoral, impractical, and it misses the higher goals of our Hebrew-Christian heritage. It is not the meaning of life. Jesus taught that those who measured life by the abundance of things had experienced the ultimate deception!

Myth 5. *We are the hope of the world. The U.S. is ordained by God to be rich and powerful. We are No. 1.*

Who doubts that the U.S. is No. 1 in power and resources? In terms of rich soil, water, timber, coal, oil, and many minerals necessary for technological development, the U.S. is preeminent. Our Gross National Product ($2,853 billions in 1980) is more than the combined GNP of Japan, Canada, the Soviet Union, all the OPEC countries, and all the Latin American countries combined.

Yet the U.S. no longer has the highest standard of living or the highest per capita income. Three or four countries have surpassed us. Nor are we first in longevity, literacy rate, low infant mortality rates, or in health care for all the people.

The U.S. is not the most generous country in the world with all of our disaster programs and the supposed aid and "give away" enterprises. At least fourteen countries give more to Third World countries than does the U.S., in terms of our ability to give (as measured by our GNP). In absolute dollars, we give more. In view of our ability to give, we are far from generous!

Surely the U.S. ranks first in industrial and agricultural productivity. No! Japan and several other countries out-produce the U.S. The sheer bulk of our production is larger; but in terms of efficiency of operation and production compared to the energies expended, we are not doing well. Even American agriculture, which produces mountains of food stuffs, is not very efficient. We spend enormous amounts of energy and involve vast amounts of valuable metals and minerals in the process.

Kenneth Boulding reminds us that there is no law of God that America should be the richest and most powerful country in the world. Surely, inestimable riches are at our disposal. But let's not call them God's blessings. God is not blind to how we use our possessions or how we got them (stolen land, exploitation of the Indians and blacks and immigrants, the eviction and practical genocide of native Americans, massive erosion and pollution).

Myth No. 6. *If people try hard enough, they can make it.*
Many good people have said of the poor: "If they had worked as hard as I have worked, they wouldn't be where they are." An aura of self-righteousness prevails. Those who haven't made it are lazy, shiftless, and weak of character. They have no perseverance and lack will. For these reasons they were not able to climb the ladder of upward mobility.

The facts are clear. About 30 million people in the U.S. are not making it; they live below the poverty level as defined by the government. In the whole world, the situation is much worse. Lester Brown says that nearly two billion are affected by caloric or protein deficiencies. About one billion face chronic malnutrition; 455 million are starving presently. In many parts of the world almost every child suffers from some form of dietary deficiency.

Actually, the poor work harder. Modern conveniences are generally lacking: running water, sewage disposal, and electricity. Hundreds of thousands walk long distances for water and firewood. The struggle for survival is a daily battle, and a losing one.

Billions of God's children live in poverty through no fault of their own. Unemployment is a daily humiliation for hundreds of millions. Vast tracts of land in the Third World have been bought by multinational corporations to produce luxury products for the rich: coffee, cocoa, pineapple, sugar, carnations, cattle, etc. Peasants lose access to the land. High technology used by gigantic corporations employs less people than previously. Unemployment increases in the countryside; people flock to the cities.

The poor do not have a fair deal. Our economic system—free enterprise capitalism—is not free. It is monopolistic; it is controlled by the few. It brings unbelievable affluence to some at the price of exploitation of the powerless poor. The great need is for the democratization of capitalism.

Preaching the doctrine of "pulling oneself up by the bootstraps" is false, cruel, and un-Christian. It is an exercise in self-righteousness. Let us be done with it!

Myth 7. *Criticism of our economic system is anti-American.*

The term anti-American is inappropriate for a number of reasons. Criticism, openness, and freedom are characterizing features of our heritage in the U.S. We cherish them. Criticism starts us on the search for alternatives, corrections, and the vigorous transformations needed. Senator Hatfield calls for a new economic system that will serve all humanity. Neither capitalism nor Soviet socialism is working well. Both are fraught with gross inequities, class distinctions, and lack of freedoms.

Common people deserve democratic control of their economic lives. Democratized capitalism would involve a climate favorable to small businesses and family farms, more common ownership of factories and businesses, more cooperatives, more people controlling both production and consumption, advertising that informs instead of manipulates, enforcement of antitrust laws and laws prohibiting monopolies, price-fixing and gobbling up the land and other resources of the world by great corporations.

Myth No. 8. *If our economy is left to itself, things will work out for the best.*

This is laissez-faire economics without embellishment.

Adam Smith stated the argument in his *Wealth of Nations.*
Smith argued that the pursuit of self-interest promotes the
best interests of society. The rich are led by an "invisible
hand" so that without their knowing it the rich engage their
energies for the general welfare. Ambitious people inadvertent-
ly do things that are economically most useful. Free actions of
individuals produce not chaos, but an orderly process in
economic affairs. We get good meat from the butcher, not from
benevolence but from his own self-interest. So Smith's
arguments go.

Smith was naive; his view of human nature was lop-sided;
his faith in privatism is unwarranted. He was blind to
catastrophic hardships accruing from unchecked self-interest.
He seems totally unaware of economic exploitation rooting in
greed. Worst of all, *he divinized power, self-interest, and
monopolistic economic practices.* He is a thousand miles away
from biblical understandings!

The Old Testament prophets saw no "invisible hand"
operating in economic affairs. They saw the rich getting richer
at the expense of the poor. Activities in the marketplace didn't
work out for the general welfare. The poor suffered at the
hands of the powerful rich.

Jesus, likewise, saw poverty, brokenness, bruisedness,
bondage, and imprisonment emerging from the unchecked free
enterprise. He knew what was in people, their greed, their exploitation of fellow humans, and their anxieties about material
security.

Churchmen of Latin America see no "invisible hand" of
God guiding the multinationals in their countries. They see
low wages, dangerous working conditions, price setting by the
powerful, and their own dictatorial governments kept in power
by U.S. training of their police and armies to protect mutual
economic interests.

Likewise, the 30 *millions* living below the poverty line in
the U.S. see no "invisible hand" working for their welfare.

Why are things not working out for the one-billion malnourished and the 455 millions who starve in our world? J. K.
Galbraith, noted economist, speaks of the myth under consideration: "Left to themselves, economic forces do not work
out for the best, except for the powerful."

Myth 9. *Security rests in greater and greater expenditures for
the military.*
The Old Testament decried this as a falsehood. Israel was
not to trust in armies, weaponry, or military alliances. Those
who trusted in the sword would perish by the sword, they said.
Jesus was a peacemaker, the Prince of Peace. He trusted in
the power of love and love alone. The armaments he used were
unending love, unlimited forgiveness, reconciliation at all
costs, turning the other cheek, and overcoming evil with good.
Finally, he laid down his life. He was strong, righteous, totally
nonviolent in his approach to evil. He taught and
demonstrated that it is better to give one's life than to take
life.
Security does not abide in armaments. Currently, the U.S.
and the U.S.S.R. have the largest death-dealing arsenals ever
devised by any nation. We have plans and capabilities to
destroy 50-100-150 millions of the purported enemy. The world
is spending about 500 billions yearly in a snowballing arms
race—about one million per minute!
Who feels secure?
The superpowers, caught in obsessive fears, short on
diplomacy and the arts of reconciliation, trust the immense
risks of the arms race and limited nuclear war rather than the
lesser risks of peacemaking.
Who feels secure?
We manufacture three to five nuclear bombs a day,
develop the MX missile system, and the B-1 bomber.
Long range plans will double the military budget by 1986.
Over 50 percent of U.S. tax dollars will be spent for all military

functions: the Department of Defense, the Pentagon, the
Veterans Administration, and the unpaid debts on past wars.

Myth 10. *The U.S. must feed the world.*

It is commonly assumed that the U.S. is the breadbasket
of the world and that if the world hunger problem is to be
solved, we must export more food. This is fallacious!

Most of our agricultural exports (56 percent) go to industrial countries. Japan, the Netherlands, West Germany, and
Canada were the chief recipients. Our present role in the world
food trade is not feeding the hungry but selling to the rich.

While the U.S. is the world's leading exporter of food, we
are also one of the world's top importers. In 1974, the U.S. was
third among the world's leading importers (close behind Japan
and West Germany). The U.S. imports 40 percent of all beef in
world trade—2 billion pounds in 1973. Over two thirds of our
imports come from underdeveloped countries. We generally
import more food from developing nations than we sell or give
to them.

Food exported on an aid basis is generally not a gift, but
sold on long-term, low interest financing. Such food aid con-
stitutes only a tiny fraction of our commercial exports (6 percent in 1975), and aid programs are decreasing).

Frances Moore Lappe and Joseph Collins, of the Institute
for Food and Development Policy, make us aware of a crucial
matter. "Every country in the world has the capacity to feed
itself," they say. We must stop asking "What can we do for
them?" Instead we must ask "What obstacles interfere with
poor people taking control of production so that they can feed
themselves?"

Actually, there is enough food in the world to feed adequately all of God's children. This was true even in the worst
famine years of the early 70s. Millions starve in sight of food.
They are poor; they cannot buy it. Poverty is the primal cause
of starvation.

It is a myth that maldistribution of food is the heart of world hunger problems. There's a bit of truth in this, but it is not a major factor. More roads, trains, and ocean transports will not resolve the major causes of world hunger.

It is a myth that overpopulation is the cause of world hunger. The most densely populated countries have virtually no starvation (The Netherlands, Belgium, Japan, West Germany, and England). The highest densities of population occur in rich developed nations. China, though not nearly as densely populated as the above named countries, has twice as many people per acre as India; yet the Chinese are not hungry, while massive hunger persists in India. There is no correlation between density of population and hunger. Nearly every country in the world can feed its own people if the people have access to the land, water, and other food-related resources.

# 6
# Contemporary
# U.S. Economy

The United States economy is based on the capitalist model. Ours is a large-scale industrial capitalism described by Paul Johnson as one "in which privately-financed publicly-quoted corporations, operating in a free market environment, and with the backup of the private enterprise money market, constitute the core of national economies."

In our economy the allocation of resources is very largely determined by the market and so we call it a market economy. As the decisions that govern economic activity are made at three different levels, we have a *mixed market economy*. The three levels are

• *Widely scattered individuals and small groups.* These are relatively limited in scope, and the decisions they make are coordinated through the mechanism of the market.

• *The giant corporations and the labor unions.* Many of the more important decisions are made at this level by giant impersonal corporations (including the multinationals) and to a lesser extent by labor unions. Corporations and certain labor unions represent a highly concentrated form of power, influence a broad segment of total economic activity, and are significantly insulated from the dictates of the market.

• *The government.* The participation of the government in economic decision making represents the political more than market imperative.

Let us now examine some of the sectors of our economy.

*The Small Businesses*

Any industrialized society pursues its economic organization through enterprise units. In our economy there are
roughly 10 million "small" businesses, counting every one
from the newsstand through the farm (1.7 million farms) up to
enterprises that employ several hundred people and count
their dollar volume in tens of millions.

There are more than 10 million legally autonomous enterprises (proprietorships), most of them comparatively small
(99.1 percent have fewer than 100 employees). They sell one or
a few products or services and compete for customers with
others of their kind on the basis of price and quality. New firms
come into the local market easily, and failures are just as common and frequent. The small enterpreneurs constitute the very
core of the American "middle class" and thus give a small-
business appearance, characteristic to much of American
political and social life.

*Corporate Giants*

The very fact that an overwhelming number of businesses
in the U.S. are small gives a deceiving appearance to the
business scene. The millions of mini-businesses do not begin to
match the economic power of a tiny number of giant enterprises at the other end of the scale. The few giants control the
great bulk of the nation's productive assets and the income
they generate belongs to a small group who reach out into all
corners of the economy. The giants constitute a core, as it
were, and small business, its periphery. A few hundred large
industrial corporations represent an economy within an
economy, controlling a third of all the tangible wealth of the
nation. All by itself, this very small core of corporations—500
at the most, including such well-known ones as Exxon, General
Motors, IBM, U.S. Steel, and RCA—accounts for two thirds of
all industrial sales. Within that core is a smaller core that by
itself produces the main flow of industrial production on which

the economy rests. The top of the pyramid is represented by the 137 largest U.S. manufacturers who in 1974 accounted for 50 percent of the manufacturing assets and 54.8 percent of the net manufacturing profits.

There are only about 3,000 companies listed on U.S. stock exchanges and another 3,000 corporations whose stock is nationally traded over the counter. In numbers, those 6,000 national companies represent 0.04 percent of the total business population of 14 million enterprises. These are the firms which are likely to have access to national financing through both equity and debt markets, and which engage in national or international marketing, nationwide advertising, and nationwide personnel recruitment. They play the most significant role in our economy.

In terms of financial turnover, the largest fifty enjoy a combined sales revenue that approaches one fourth of America's gross national product. Exxon alone employs 175,000 workers worldwide (86,813 in the U.S. in 1980) and its sales revenue exceeds $100 billion, more than the GNP of such countries as the Union of South Africa, Denmark, Austria, Yugoslavia, Turkey, and Norway.

Generally speaking, the two segments—the small businesses and the giants—function independently of each other, competing basically with their own kind. However, through mergers or quasi-mergers with large enterprises, a sizeable number of small concerns loses its independence each year. They become subsidiaries of the giants by formally merging assets with them. Many more are subsidiaries in all but name. Those holding franchises or dealerships, for all practical purposes, are transformed into agents of the great corporations; others are tightly bound by contracts or reciprocal buying agreements. This being the reality, although price and product competition persist throughout the economy, the rivalry is increasingly among the few rather than the many. The giants, while exposed in some degree to market forces, have considerable latitude in what goods and services to produce, what price to charge, and so on. With large resources at their command, the giants can diversify production, operate plants at a number of different locations at home and abroad, and also decide which plants are closed and where new ones are to be opened. In other words, the giant corporations have enormous economic as well as political power and, therefore, have control over the lives of millions of workers who depend on them.

Twenty-five years ago, five hundred American corporations controlled more than half of all of the country's assets. Six years ago, two hundred corporations owned more than half the assets. In 1981, fifty corporations controlled over 42 percent of all assets.

*The Labor Sector*

According to 1980 figures of the Bureau of Labor statistics, 106.8 million men and women are in the labor force, defined as all those of working age who are gainfully employed or actively seeking paid employment. Of the nearly 107 million Americans who must work for a living, about 100 million, when they can find jobs, work for someone else. This situation drives home the point that capitalism came into being when labor (as opposed to merely labor's products) became a commodity, a thing bought and sold in the market. Along with raw materials, machinery, and other commodities, labor itself becomes an element needed for production of useful goods and services.

Workers in our economy enjoy a very large degree of freedom of occupational choice and mobility to suit personal preferences. Within the boundaries of this freedom, entrance to many occupations is partially closed by educational, experiential, or licensing requirements. Economic individualism prevails in the allocation of labor resources in the United States.

Wage rates (the price of labor) are generally determined by

the interplay of market forces. Institutional factors, chiefly labor unions, significantly influence both the demand for and supply of labor. Overall, unions represent only 22.4 million workers, or 20.9 percent of the total American labor force. This certainly is rather low and perhaps indicative of problems confronting the labor movement in the U.S. But then, it must be remembered that America's business is business; and that business, not labor, signifies the American character.

Unionism is fairly strongly established in some of the major manufacturing, transportation, and communications industries. However, it is weak and faltering in many others.

New areas of employment often utilize sophisticated techniques based on computers and telecommunications. The nature of these jobs and the training and sophistication of some the workers in the service industries, among other factors, have contributed to the labor movement's lack of success in organizing these workers.

The structure of employment in the 1970s has also changed significantly. The 1970s were a time of rapid expansion of employment. Almost 13 million jobs were added, 11 million of which were in the private sector of the economy. The new jobs were concentrated in services and in retail trade, making these two sectors responsible for the employment of 43 percent of all Americans employed in the private nonagricultural economy by 1979. The two sectors together provided more than 70 percent of all new private jobs created from 1973 to the summer of 1980.

The three industries which provided more than a million new jobs each during the 1973-79 period were "eating and drinking places," including fast food restaurants; "health services," including private hospitals, nursing homes, and doctors' and dentists' offices; and "business services," including personnel supply services, reproduction and mailing, and services to buildings. These industries provided employment sixteen times faster than the goods-producing, or industrial, sector of the economy.

This new trend has profound consequences for the organization of American society and for the American economy. We seem to be moving toward a structure of employment ever more dominated by jobs that are badly paid, unchanging, and unproductive. The shift in employment from high to low productivity sectors of the economy is likely to slow the rate of growth of productivity which is presently one of our major economic problems.

One of the significant outcomes of the new trend is that the new industries provide employment for women. Women accounted for 41 percent of all employment in 1979 and 31 percent of all manufacturing employment. Women also accounted for 56 percent of all people employed in eating and drinking places, 43 percent of employment in business services (a sharp increase since the early 1970s), and 81 percent of employment in health services.

*The Government Sector*

In spite of labels such as "free enterprise," "free market economy," and others, we cannot escape the reality that the U.S. government plays a key role, perhaps a dominant role, in the nation's economy. Our economy is a good example of the role the public sector plays in creating an economic climate in which the private sector can flourish and make economic progress. Governmental intervention influences what and how much is produced, how it will be produced, and how it will be shared and used without leaving such decisions exclusively to free market forces.

Governmental intervention in the economy is not a new phenomenon for us. The economy has never been totally free of it. Since the early days of the Republic, governmental regulations have been introduced now and then for keeping in check the activities of private corporations. Deeper governmental involvement, however, began with the Great Depression and little has changed since that time. Governmental participation is bigger now than at any other time in the history of the nation. Our government has played a major role in leading American industries in agriculture, aeronautics, nuclear power, electronics, computers, communications, genetic engineering, and other emerging technologies.

Our government influences the allocation of resources in several ways—through production control over certain items needed for national defense; through highway construction; through regulation and controls to ensure the free play of market forces; and through taxation, spending, and redistribution of income among individuals. We will examine the governmental activity in the economy under three major headings: public enterprises; taxes, purchases, transfer payments, money, and credit; and direct regulation.

*Public Enterprise.* Public enterprise carries little economic weight, accounting for little over 1 percent of GNP and employing less than 2 percent of the nation's workers. There are about 18,000 public enterprises in the U.S., including public authorities and special districts. Most of them are local or regional in scope, but a few operate nationwide, and even these are much smaller than the nation's largest corporations. Tennessee Valley Authority, Port of New York Authority, and the U.S. Postal Service are examples of some of these large public enterprises.

*Taxes, purchases, and transfer payments.* Taxes are responsible for nearly 90 percent of the current revenue of all levels of government combined. Nearly one third of the gross national product (GNP) in the United States is taken in taxes by federal, state, and local governments. Of this amount one third is returned in transfer payments: social insurance and welfare benefits, veterans' benefits, subsidies to private enterprises, and interest on the national debt. The remaining two thirds is used to buy goods and services: military personnel and supplies, police and fire protection, educational supplies, and services.

Purchases of goods and services by the federal, state, and local governments currently account for about one fourth of the GNP. Voters, not the marketplace, have control of this resource. Nearly all the goods and services in question must be produced by government and paid for with tax revenues. Can you imagine what would happen if the federal, state, and local governments suddenly withdrew their share of the economy, reducing it by almost $17 billion?

About 10 percent of the GNP goes toward transfer payments to individuals, groups, and institutions that are not currently providing productive service in return. These payments include veterans benefits, old-age pensions, public assistance (welfare) benefits, subsidies to merchant shipping and airlines, educational opportunity grants, rent supplements, tax credits, and agricultural subsidies. The payments are often made in kind rather than in cash, for example, health care services provided without charge or at a price below cost of supply.

*Regulation.* Direct governmental intervention in American economic life takes several forms. In certain cases private consumption is subjected to public control—examples: narcotics, pornographic movies, etc. For health and safety, certain requirements, like seat belts in cars, avoidance of products suspected of causing cancer and so on, are enforced.

Governmental regulation of specific kinds of business has also increased over the years. Statutory commissions exercise control over prices and standards of service in the areas of electric power, telecommunications, and rail transport. State and local boards and commissions also regulate prices, wage rates, or working conditions.

In the depression era, during Roosevelt's first two terms, which spanned most of the lean years, ninety-three pieces of major legislation were passed that directly and often permanently affected banking, business, agriculture, labor, and social welfare. More important than the New Deal legislation, as such, was the fact that it only set the stage for the role government would be playing a generation later. However, without governmental intervention during the Great Depression the economy would have collapsed totally. The government's role then, as now, has basically been to help the private sector of the economy stay in business, particularly in those areas where profits are to be made.

The U.S. government on various occasions has also resorted to price and wage controls. The most recent example was during the Nixon administration's efforts to enforce an "income policy" through a three-month "freeze" on prices and wage rates followed by certain other restrictions.

*Strengths of Our Economy*

Having gained a general idea of how our economy is organized and the role of various sectors in it, let us turn our attention to some of the strengths of our economic system. At this point we shall do this strictly from a utilitarian perspective, that is, on grounds of *usefulness* rather than *rightness*. We do so, because the economy of which we are an inseparable part has, for the past one hundred and fifty years, been based on the utilitarian ethic whose predominant operative moral principles have been individual satisfaction of rational desire and the notion of voluntary exchange. What then are the major successes of our economic arrangement?

1. Industrial capitalism has raised the material well-being of the masses of citizens in the advanced societies of the world to levels that were never dreamed possible. This came about in spite of the large increase in population over the last two hundred years. Masses have been delivered from grinding poverty and privation by harnessing the energy of private self-interest, and there has been a decline in absolute poverty.

2. The accumulation of wealth generated by the system has made possible the growth of educational, charitable, and philanthropic institutions. These, in turn, have provided the

additional means for research in various fields, advances in educational and social programs, as well as the extension of aid to the needy.

3. A vast middle class has come into existence and there has been a wider sharing and distribution of the fruits of created wealth.

4. The market system performs a coordinating function which would otherwise fall upon government planners.

5. The system undergirds the ideals of efficiency and freedom. Persons can establish business, seek appropriate employment, and have the freedom and opportunity for lateral and vertical movement on the economic scale.

6. The advocates of market capitalism say that capitalism works as well as it does in part because it decentralizes power and responsibility. For them, substantial economic inequality is justifiable for the preservation and enhancement of our cultural and intellectual heritage.

7. Since the early 19th century, we have approximately doubled our per capita real income every generation. This has been accompanied by a steady rise in the proportion of national income going to labor, 40 percent in the 19th century and 80 percent today. Special historical circumstances—plenty of free land and other natural resources, such as temperate climate and ample water supply—favored such rapid progress. The situation is quite different now, and it calls for new vision and new structures.

*Weaknesses of Our Economy*

What are some of the failures and problem areas of our economy?

1. Failure to control depression and unemployment is seen, particularly in the Great Depression of the 1930s when unemployment went up to 25 percent.

2. Since the 1970s, the failure to solve the inflation-unemployment dilemma has been evident.

3. The inability to prevent businesses from getting bigger and bigger creates difficulties for small businesses and other small operators and concentrates wealth and power in a few hands.

4. Failure to change the proportional distribution of income since the 1930s has resulted in a vastly unequal distribution of income and wealth. These statistics illustrate the inequity: the top one percent of American families have about as much after-tax income as nearly all families in the bottom 20 percent; the top fifth of families have about as much after-tax income as the bottom three-fifths. The richest one percent of American families have about one-third of all wealth and the bottom half of all families hold only 5 percent of total wealth. The top two percent of U.S. families owns about three quarters of all corporate stocks.

5. Economic discrimination based on race and sex.

6. The "economy of scale" leads to largeness of organizations which in turn leads to alienation in the workplace and to insensitivity to the values of participation.

7. The overall tax system is not very progressive. Large corporations get much bigger tax breaks and advantage than smaller ones or wage earners.

8. A substantial proportion of the gross national product goes to the war industry, from about 0.6 percent in the 1930s to about 9 percent today. This misallocation diverts valuable resources to unproductive purposes.

9. The public grants economy which uses about 10 percent of the gross national product is not well coordinated and guided, with the consequences that a good deal of the redistribution goes to the rich instead of those who need it most.

10. There is considerable amount of waste and environmental degradation.

The next chapters will examine several specific segments of our economy in greater detail.

# 7
# Guns and Butter

This chapter takes a look at two specific areas of the contemporary U.S. economy: military production and the food industry.

## I. The Military Economy

The government has become an integral part of the economy, and it is no exaggeration to say that without it, the economy cannot function. A large part of the dependency upon government relates to the needs of the military which have made the government the largest single source of demand since 1941. The government's economic activity is thus centered around military production, or the "war industry," which is that part of the economy purchased by military budgets. The share of the war industry has varied over the last fifty years from 0.6 percent of the Gross National Product (GNP) to about 42 percent in 1944. In 1980 it was running at about 9.5 percent of GNP but dramatic increases are projected through 1986.

The 1980 U.S. military budget, representing roughly one quarter of all federal spending, totalled $223 billion. Included in that figure are national defense and other military-related outlays. How did our economy come to have such a large military sector? We did have an enormous military production in World War II, but the general assumption was that after the war we would disarm ourselves. Also present was another assumption: that disarming could lead to a depression. At the time most analyses pointed to military spending as the only solution to avoid a depression. The cold war began in this kind of an atmosphere, and it may be helpful to examine its possible relationship to our military economy.

By the late 1940s it was becoming clear that the Soviet Union intended to maintain its own sphere of influence over Eastern Europe. Certain events in 1949-50 signalling the emergence of the Soviets as a competing power alarmed the State Department policy planners. This factor together with the slowdown of the U.S. economy in 1949 and 1950 was the context in which the policy of containment militarism was formulated. The classified position paper (recently declassified) describing the policy was known as National Security Council Document 68 (NSC-68). It was the adoption of the proposals of NSC-68 that led to the expenditure of over $2 trillion for the military in the 1950-72 period. NSC-68 became the planning document for the early cold war.

The cold war continues to this day and our military economy keeps expanding. Despite the cold-war rhetoric of the last three decades, the two major powers have never clashed militarily but have operated chiefly through surrogates or through "war by proxy." The obvious conclusion, therefore, is that the armament spending justified by the cold-war rhetoric was not necessary from a military point of view. It had other goals. The goals, as evidenced from the U.S. military roles in different areas of the world since the end of World War II, are primarily economic in nature, that is, to protect U.S. investments abroad and the economy at home. We could conclude, therefore, that the foundation of the U.S. militarism is economic, not ideological.

*Who Makes Decisions?*
In the two world wars the industrialists dictated to

the government how the procurement process should be run, dominated the Department of Defense (DOD), and made huge profits. The situation has continued ever since but is more sophisticated now.

The decisions now are made by a defense policy apparatus called the "Iron Triangle," consisting of the Pentagon, the defense industry, and the armed services and military appropriations committees in Congress. This small group decides what weapons will be made before they are even on the drawing boards in research and development labs. The Iron Triangle sets the priorities that are ultimately reflected in the defense budget. The defense industry manufactures the weapons which the DOD needs and wants, and the Congressional committees approve the funding for them. So the three sides of the triangle work closely and harmoniously together.

A very harmonious relationship also exists between the public and private sectors of the defense community. The defense contractors do extensive lobbying in Washington to get policies and procurement decisions favorable to them. Practically every state in the union has military procurement contracts of one kind or another which provide jobs. Defense contractors' employees, the communities where the companies are located, the stockholders, subcontractors, and suppliers are all part of the defense-contract network and may indeed depend on it for survival. Leading labor unions have members who work in defense industries. When called upon by companies to support particular weapons systems, representatives from their locals lobby in Washington. Members of Congress also have an interest in the welfare of their consituents employed in defense-related industries. With all these interest and power groups working together it is not surprising that the defense budget keeps escalating.

The U.S. Department of Defense is the largest planned economy in the world today outside the Soviet Union. It spends more than the net income of all U.S. corporations put together. By 1969 it had 470 major and 6,000 lesser installations, owned 39 million acres of land, spent over $80 billion a year, used 22,000 primary contractors and 100,000 subcontractors—thus directly employing in the armed forces and military production about 10 percent of the U.S. labor force, that is, approximately 10 million people.

Normally, what we read about is the national defense segment which represents 5 percent of GNP. However, the total outlay jumps up to 9.5 percent of GNP, which is pretty nearly double. When expenditure is labeled "national defense" and thus is expressed as a percent of GNP, it draws away attention from several facts:

• That 6.4 million U.S. workers are employed by the military either in uniform, as civilians, as military plant workers, or as reserves;

• That perhaps as many as 825,000 workers are engaged in the $15 billion arms export market;

• That military-related research employs roughly one third of all scientists and research engineers and absorbs two thirds of all research funds allocated by the federal government.

*Effects on the Economy*

What are the effects of high military expenditures on the domestic economy?

High military expenditures contribute to inflation. By putting money in the hands of workers, it creates demand for consumer goods but it also produces goods which cannot be recycled into the economy (missiles, bombs, etc.). Therefore, the price of consumer goods—like autos, refrigerators, and machine tools—goes up. Secondly, the production of military goods also increases the scarcity of material and human resources. Military contracts operate on a cost-plus basis, thus reducing the incentive to control costs. Such contracts tend to bid up the prices of resources and skilled labor, thereby feeding the inflation in the rest of the economy.

Military expenditures aggravate unemployment. By feeding industries that are so capital-intensive, military spending creates fewer jobs than an equivalent amount of civilian spending would. Moreover the jobs created in the defense sector are generally unstable and disproportionately highly skilled because modern arms have a high level of technological sophistication.

Military expenditures tend to undermine the health of the civilian sector of the economy. Money and talent that go into military uses are not available for improving industrial plants and for vital services such as clean water, reliable transportation, and so on. Thus the indispensable underpinnings for an industrial system are neglected.

Higher military expenditures increase military influence in the political process. Most major defense contractors maintain offices in Washington, D.C. and hire lobbyists to look after their special interests. We also find that defense contractors use the political action committees by making contributions to them for the election of members of Congress.

Finally, military expenditures decrease security in the long run, nationally and internationally. They create the constant risk of war, even nuclear war, and provoke small wars at local levels. They also encourage militarization of the planet with a result that much-needed resources are diverted from developmental programs to destructive and unproductive uses.

Is it possible to change things around without a major economic dislocation? Experience in other places indicates that it is possible. Obviously, in such an effort, our federal government will have to bear the major responsibility for such conversion.

A U.S. government study found that a 30-percent cut in defense spending would create an estimated 2.1 million new jobs if the conversions were carefully targeted to the right programs. Many bills dealing with the conversion process have been placed before the U.S. Senate, and the Office of Economic

Adjustment was created to deal with the issue. If our government and people are ready, a change from a largely military-based economy to a productive civilian economy can be brought about.

## II. THE FOOD INDUSTRY

Food is our biggest business. Food costs, like other living expenses, have risen considerably in recent years and continue to go up. While this is true, it is only fair to point out that, on an average, Americans spend a considerably smaller proportion of their disposable income on food as compared to consumers in other countries. Also, the food dollar in America can purchase an amazing variety of edibles. However, all is not well with the U.S. food system.

The base of the American economy has been agriculture. The achievements of U.S. agriculture, taken for granted for the past half century, remain the unseen basis of much of American prosperity. The pattern of industrial development has historically been determined by the ability of the American economy to solve the agricultural "problem." Cheap food and clothing enabled the blue-collar and white-collar workers to spend the greater part of their income on homes, cars, appliances, and other durable goods.

When we speak of the production of food, we generally refer to agriculture. The concept of a *food system* is an inclusive concept which broadens our understanding of the various processes which are exceedingly sophisticated and energy intensive. In fact, what happens in this system is that one series of industrial products are transformed into another series of industrial products which happen to be edible.

Susan George, in a helpful book *Feeding the Few,* suggests that our food system can be visualized as a line or a chain with three segments—*inputs, food production,* and *post-harvest (storage, processing, and distribution).* In the agrarian economies, the chain tends to be very short, the three segments mostly localized, and the producers and consumers are the same people. The chain in the U.S., however, is quite long because industry has taken over the provision of all the agricultural inputs and because the storage, processing, and distribution are immensely sophisticated operations, costing two thirds of every dollar spent on food. Let us examine each of these segments briefly.

*Input.* American farmers now spend over $85 billion a year on manufactured inputs, and they are totally dependent on industry for every item that goes into food production. Farm indebtedness has been skyrocketing since 1973, and it continues to escalate while real farm incomes keep declining. Bankruptcies are common. The reduction in the number of farms in the last fifty years is a good indicator of what has been happening. The number has gone down from 6.8 million in 1930 to around 2 million now, and the downward trend will continue unless drastic measures are taken by the federal government.

Large or small, farmers are more and more in the hands of their bankers, who help them to stay afloat or to expand. Generally the banks exercise stringent control and many times even prescribe what to plant, how much to plant, what fertilizer to use, and so on. Why are farmers constantly dependent on outside sources of money? One important reason is that, more and more, the farmer has to buy most of his input and supplies in less than free market conditions. Most tractors, implements, chemicals, milking machines, and veterinary medicines, to name a few items, come from economically concentrated suppliers. For example, John Deere and International Harvester, between them, control 60 percent of the farm machinery market. Corn seed is another example where two companies supply more than half the seed for the 68 million acres of corn in the U.S.

Another area related to input is agricultural research. Most agricultural research is carried out directly by agribusiness companies or by universities working for them or for the United States Department of Agriculture under contract. It is not surprising, therefore, that the research is geared toward what would be most beneficial for the companies. For example, a greater use of chemicals would receive a higher priority over the biological method of crop protection.

*Food Production.* This segment of the food system includes the actual farmers. Some of them may be millionaires in terms of land and equipment owned but the vast majority make less than $40,000 a year in gross sales. They also keep fewer and fewer dollars.

As the costs of production have kept going up and up, the American farmer has become dependent upon banks for survival. Just after World War II, 50 to 55 percent of a farmer's earnings went into next year's production costs. That figure now is 80 to 85 percent. One reason for the high increase is higher energy costs. But perhaps a more important reason is the trend toward a monopolization in agribusiness leading to less competition and more freedom in price-setting.

A sobering outcome of the general trend in farming is that very few young people are able to go into farming. The average investment per worker (including the owner-operator) in agriculture is now more than $400,000, or approximately ten times the amount it takes to create a job in industry.

The farmers' segment of the chain is shortest. It represents less than 3 percent of the total U.S. population living on about two million farms.

*Storage, Processing, and Distribution.* This segment of the food system includes what happens to food between the time it leaves the farm and reaches the consumer. It is the longest portion of the chain. It also represents the most added value (cost) and is the one that agribusiness is attempting everyday to make even longer.

An *oligopoly,* according to economists, exists if 55 percent or more of a given market is controlled by four or fewer companies. The enormous diversity in product labels on the supermarket shelves hides the fact of oligopoly control from the consumer. A company like Beatrice Foods (number 37 on Fortunes 1981 list of "500") with annual sales of $8.3 billion markets 8,000 different products and has bought up over four hundred companies in the past twenty-five years. The top fifty food-processing companies make about three fourths of all the profits in the industry.

Every major food category in the U.S. is under oligopoly control. In milling, the top four firms hold 75 percent of the market; for bakery products the figure is 65 percent; fluid milk, 60 percent and milk products, 70 percent; processed meats, 56 percent; bananas, 85 percent; and all canned goods, 80 percent. For canned soups, Campbells alone controls about 90 percent of the market. In the breakfast food industry, four food companies hold over 90 percent of the market.

One of the biggest changes in the food industry since World War II has been the drive toward vertical integration. This term simply means that individual companies attempt to control as many segments of the chain as they possibly can. Some buy up seed companies, or institutional feeding operations, or supermarkets, or chains of restaurants. One form of vertical integration is contract farming in which the company holds farmers under contract to plant certain crops and to sell only to the company at a fixed price.

Highest integration is in vegetables for processing (95 percent); fresh-market vegetables (51 percent); citrus fruits (85 percent); potatoes (70 percent); fluid milk (98 percent); broilers (97 percent); seed crops (80 percent); and sugar (100 percent). The crops still being sold on the open market in overwhelming proportions were food and feed grains, cotton, tobacco, oil-seed crops, and livestock (excluding chickens). If the trends of the last decade in vertical integration continue, it is estimated that by 1985, 75 percent of the entire U.S. food supply will be produced through vertical integration or under contract to a food firm.

*Some Areas of Concern*

The preceding analysis raises a number of concerns which call for thoughtful deliberation and perhaps action. Our food system is based on a shaky foundation. Its economic structure consisting of price supports, tax write-offs, emergency loan programs, and artificially inflated land values is feeble, to say the least. Without these props, many U.S. farmers would be bankrupt right now and many are just about in that position.

The perilous course our food system has been on for sometime now will lead to a still higher concentration of control in the hands of a few corporations. This would then mean that these few corporations would have complete and unchallenged control over not only what we eat but also over what we pay for it. This could happen, not by some malicious design, but as a result of an evolving economic process, unchallenged by public awareness. A heavy price has already been paid in the past through the loss of family farms, small food processors, and local grocery stores. The price continues to be paid in the destruction of rural communities, soil erosion and the depletion of nonrenewable resources.

# 8
# Communication and Small Business

Two additional segments of our economy are examined in this chapter, the communications industry and small businesses.

## I. The Media

We live in a world dominated by its means of communication. In that world, we receive information from a variety of systems and sources, including newspapers and magazines, books and magnetic tapes, films, records, radio, television, and cable and satellite transmissions. Collectively they represent what is commonly known as media. We shall deal here with a few noteworthy characteristics of our media.

Our media are channels of communication and information. But they are also industries dealing with products and profits. Our communication system is commercial in nature and is privately owned within the context of the First Amendment. Certain regulatory functions are performed by the federal government, mainly through the Federal Communications Commission. The profit motivation is just as strong in this sector of the economy as in others. An important question is, how extensive are federal regulations, and how adequate are they for ensuring objectivity of information?

None of us controls the media experience. Media products are written, produced, and directed by others. Therefore, what we receive, especially from the all-pervasive "mass media," is their version of the world, and that version may be quite different from the world as it actually exists in our collective consciousness. As a result, the people who use a medium impose their own values and biases on the audience.

Newspapers are no longer the prime source of news for most Americans. According to yearly Roper polls, television has been the major news medium for a majority of the country since 1974. It is expected that television will remain in prime position for quite a while yet, although the rise of cable and videodisc could alter its shape significantly.

*Media Conglomerates*

James Monaco points out that twelve media conglomerates had total net sales in 1976 equal to half of the net sales for all media; and the "revenue from media operations for the twelve represents thirty percent of net sales for all media and fifty percent of sales for all nonprint media." His compilation for 1976, summarized below, clearly shows the trend toward the concentration of media control in a few hands.

• *Newspapers.* The ten largest newspaper chains account for 51 percent of total newspaper revenues of $11.2 billion. The fifty largest newspaper chains have more than two thirds of all subscribers.

• *Records.* Warner Communications, Inc. and CBS, Inc. receive approximately 65 percent of all record and tape wholesale revenues in the United States.

• *Television.* The three commercial networks, ABC, CBS, and NBC, account for 69 percent of total television revenue. Eighty-five percent of commercial television stations are affiliated with one or another of the three networks. Twenty-two cable operators cover 51 percent of the market.

• *Films.* In any year, three of the top five distributors receive more than half of film rental revenues. In 1976 Warner Bros., United Artists, and Twentieth Century Fox accounted for 48 percent of total rental revenues; in 1975 Universal, Fox, and Columbia accounted for 52 percent of total rental revenues.

• *Nonprint.* In any year, six media companies—ABC, NBC, CBS, Warner Communications, Inc. (WCI), and any two other film companies—control more than half of each of the nonprint media markets in the U.S.

Monaco observes that nonprint media are solidly oligopolistic and the print media are rapidly approaching that state.

The trend toward mergers, consolidation, and conglomeration is applicable to media in the same manner as is commonly found for most other U.S. industries. There is a growing vertical control of information and cross-media ownership, not just between newspapers and broadcast stations but among magazines and book publishers. A good illustration of this is found in the activities of the RCA Corporation which now owns the following kinds of businesses:

• *Broadcasting.* Owns NBC and five of the most powerful VHF television stations.

• *Electronics.* Consumer electronics (color television sets, radios, videocassette recorders, etc.), Selecta Vision videodiscs, solid-state components, picture tubes, distributor and special products, government and commercial systems, and RCA Service Company.

• *Communications.* RCA Global Communications, an international cable-and-radio-communications service; and Random House, a major book publisher (and subsidiaries of Random House, such as Ballantine Books, Alfred Knopf, Pantheon, Vintage, and Modern Library.)

• *Diversified Business.* Banquet Foods; Coronet Industries, a carpet and home furnishings manufacturer; Cusham and Wakefield, a real-estate concern; Hertz, the leading automobile renter; and Oriel Foods.

Listings could be made for other media-related corporations as well. For example, CBS Inc. owns, among other things, Holt, Rinehart, and Winston publishing groups, *Field*

& *Stream* magazine, *Road & Track*, *World Tennis*, and *Cycle World* plus the former Fawcett Magazines.

The preceding paragraphs raise many questions and concerns. It is, therefore, important for us to look at mass media. We experience mass media everyday. They set the agenda for our daily consideration of issues and problems which they present to us. Mass media, particularly mass electronic media, assume special relevance and significance for us as Christian citizens as well as for the church. We will focus mainly on television because of its pervasiveness (98 percent of American homes have television sets) and the persuasiveness of its messages.

*The Role of Television*

In the average household, Americans watch television for nearly 6½ hours per day. When we think about the role of television in our lives, the first thing that comes to mind is television advertising. We are constantly bombarded by costly advertising. Some estimates inform us that the average teenager has watched 350,000 commercials before leaving high school. Over $10 billion are spent every year on television advertising for selling products for our consumption. The unit costs of some television commercials are mind boggling. For example, "60 Minutes" (the highest priced show at $175,000 per 30 seconds), "MASH" and "Dallas" carry prices over $100,000 per 30 seconds. What's in it for CBS? On a weekly basis, CBS' average prime time ad revenues are on the order of $29.7 million. Similar data can be provided for ABC and NBC as well. Advertising is highly profitable for the commercial television networks. But the real question is, what does advertising do to us?

Advertising brings the highly paid salesperson right into our living rooms to persuade us that material possessions will bring joy and fulfillment. It attempts constantly to appeal to acquisitiveness in contradistinction to our Christian understanding that affluence does not guarantee love, acceptance, and joy. Advertising then challenges our values and works relentlessly at undermining them, and we may be won over if we are not alert and analytical. The larger question to consider is, can we and our society survive very long in view of the fact that one of our central institutions, namely advertising, is based on the advocacy of unrestrained greed?

*Public Access*

This brings us to the second area of concern which deals with public access to television broadcasting. We have referred to the oligopolistic control of the TV networks. We know that transmission and subscription costs are very high and that capital is a significant factor. The present technology of television broadcasting, based on the use of electromagnetic spectrum, limits the number of channels available to users. If cable transmission becomes as widespread as television broadcasting is at the present time and if the cable systems are allowed to develop as common carriers, many channels may be available, and access could be broadened. But that is still in the future. Up until now the issue of public access has not received the serious attention it deserves.

Public access assumes importance if we value democratic processes and the diversity of information sources promised us by the First Amendment. As with other economic activities, television and other media focus on production and distribution aspects. Since media produce and distribute information about reality, distortion of information is a distinct possibility. As matters stand now, we cannot talk back to media. The hope that we may be able to do so lies in diversification and decentralization of media. However, the record of public television broadcasting, for a variety of reasons, has been inadequate and unsatisfactory, and the control over existing distribution patterns is oligopolistic. Therefore, the issue of public access to television becomes vital and the one for us to consider working on.

## II. SMALL BUSINESSES

Large corporations are so pervasive in our economy that we tend to forget our small businesses. However, from the earliest colonial times, small business has been the heart and soul of America. Small business owners had become "the forgotten people of American society" in the post-World War II period, but since 1975 the interest in small businesses has been revived. Small businesses have been growing at a phenomenal rate, bringing the total number of self-employed people now to an all-time high of more than 6.8 million. Two important reasons for this change are that more people from the baby boom period are looking for work now and that our economy is shifting from a manufacturing to a service-oriented economy. A third reason could be that there is a resurgence of a spirit of independence, self-reliance, and risk taking.

Of the 14 million U.S. businesses, over 10 million are classified as small businesses. The Thirty-First Annual Report of the Senate Small Business Committee, published in December 1980, lists several important contributions of small firms to our economy.

*Innovation.* One half of all commercial innovations have consistently originated with small firms and individual investors. Furthermore, the National Science Foundation has found that small firms produce innovation very efficiently. Their smallest category (less than 1,000 employees) incurs one fourth the cost per innovation of medium-sized firms (1,000 to 10,000 employees) and one twenty-fourth the cost of larger firms (over 10,000 employees).

*Economic growth.* Since economists estimate that 40 to 50 percent of economic growth is based on innovation, small firms are the source of 20 to 25 percent of national growth.

*Employment.* Fifty-five percent of all existing jobs in the private sector are in "small business" as defined by the Small Business Administration (59 percent, if farming is included). Small businesses generate the majority of new jobs. According to a study performed at the Massachusetts Institute of Technology, 52 percent of the net jobs between 1960 and 1976 were created by independent businesses with less than 20 employees.

*The quality of life.* Numerous studies establish that local businesses are a prime source of strength for their neighborhoods and communities and are the repository of many of the most deeply held American values, such as independence, individuality, and economic opportunity. The craftmanship, dedication, and human scale of small enterprise make a very real difference in the quality of American life.

*Competition.* New and small businesses are natural agents of competition. The wisdom of fostering competition through small business is apparent in the American marketplace. The products and services of most of the leading technology firms, for the most part, were unknown twenty or thirty years ago. Emerging business patterns such as employee and community ownership also offer new opportunities for broadening participation in our enterprise system.

*Problems of Small Business*

Small businesses have a high rate of failure. As many as three out of four new enterprises fail within their first five years, and nine out of ten fail within ten years. And the failures are believed to be increasing to a higher rate than at any time during the past decade.

There are many roadblocks in the way of small entrepreneurs. The biggest is finding the money to start the business. A recent poll by the National Federation of Independent Business on the most important source of financing found that 45 percent financed their business from personal savings, 13 percent from friends, while four percent cited private investors. Only 29 percent were financed through banks and other financial institutions, while one percent were financed by the government. Less than one percent obtained financing through the few venture-capital firms who are in business to make funds available to new enterprises.

A second problem which results in a high failure rate is that small businesses have no place to turn for reliable information or technical management assistance. The private business owner today has to operate in an environment where technology is applied to the marketplace but does not have the backing of research, development, and technical services which large companies have and can afford to have.

A third problem area is the enormous hassle of government regulation and paper work. This has a crippling effect on small businesses. Regulations designed for large corporations are often applied inflexibly to smaller enterprises as well. For example, a small surface mining company owner with 25 employees had to deal with 647 forms per year and a total of 63 different inspectors.

Fewer tax benefits is a fourth problem area. Small business enjoys far fewer tax benefits than big business. Internal Revenue Service figures show that companies with more than $1 billion in sales are claiming various tax credits equal to 61.1 percent of their tax liability, while comparatively small firms—those with $1 million to $5 million in sales—are claiming credits equal to only 6.5 percent. Some rules which could benefit the small firm are so complicated that they cannot afford the accounting staff to take advantage of them.

### Signs of Hope

In spite of these problems, the encouraging sign is that small business is being heard now, and it is pooling its resources to take advantage of the favorable climate prevailing in the country for small business. A number of organizations (e.g., The Council of Small Enterprises) have come into being and are providing effective services to their members.

The private sector has also come up with some innovative programs. For example, Control Data Corporation has opened four Business and Technology Centers in St. Paul, Minn., Minneapolis, Charleston, S.C., and Toledo, Ohio. The centers provide office space and a wide array of services to young, growing companies. Rent-paying tenants make use of conference rooms, mail processing, and legal consulting, as well as advice on inventory financing and tax consulting.

The spirit of free enterprise and competition seems to be making a comeback in an economy which is largely dominated by oligopolies and monopolies and restricted competition. Whether the revival of small business will help resolve some of our basic economic problems or not is difficult to predict. But under the present economic structure, small business is vital to big business. For example, General Motors has 30,500 suppliers of whom a large number are small enterprises with fewer than 500 employees.

The free market system exalted by Adam Smith assumes that the people participating in the market had some human decencies, some respect for law, some ethical habits. He presupposed a moral base, but the competitive forces released by the free market erode that base. The question then is, if free enterprise and competition are now being restored, can our social system work without some internalized altruistic norms of behavior?

# 9
# The Economy Impacts
# Creation and Education

## I. OUR ENVIRONMENT

Humans are a part of God's created order and our well-being is affected by the well-being of the rest of creation. Therefore, we should be concerned for the maintenance of the full diversity of created things. We are concerned not only because creation is good but also because the great variety of living things make up an irreplaceable genetic reservoir from which to draw new sources of food and other materials in the future. Christians have strong biblical reasons, even a mandate, for developing a way of life which treats the rest of creation with great care.

A new element in the discussion of economic systems and problems is the issue of environment. The issue is based upon growing alarm over the results of rapid industrial expansion based on modern technology. The environmental movement generally confines itself to concern over the vast and seemingly unavoidable destruction of the natural environment (i.e. the pollution of air, land, water) and the wasteful depletion of nonrenewable natural resources. Wilderness and species preservation, however, along with health and safety factors in industrial production, also come within the purview of the movement.

The basic thesis of the environmentalists is that the earth is a spaceship with finite resources and environment. Therefore, the concept of a maximum-growth economy, which assumes inexhaustible resources, an unlimited capability of nature to absorb waste and pollution, and the indestructibility of natural environment, is untenable. In other words, infinite economic growth is not possible in a finite world. Neither capitalist nor the socialist economies can expand continually without risking the possibility of a total collapse in the future. We must, therefore, come to terms with nature and its limitations.

Our indiscriminate use of natural resources for reaching and maintaining ever-rising living standards has left behind mountains of waste, poisoned rivers, smog-ridden cities, unsanitary dumps, and polluted beaches. What is the economic impact of environmental degradation? A number of examples could be given, and we will mention a few to illustrate the point. Acid rain is a commonly known example. *The Environment* magazine (May 1980) had this to say about acid precipitation.

> As a result of the combustion of tremendous quantities of fossil fuels, such as coal and oil, the United States annually discharges 50 million metric tons of sulfur and nitrogen oxides into the atmosphere. Through a series of complex chemical reactions, these pollutants may be converted into acids which may return to earth as components of either rain or snow. This acid precipitation, more commonly known as acid rain, may have severe ecological impacts on wide-spread areas of environment.

> Hundreds of lakes in North America and Scandinavia have become so acidic that they can no longer support fish life. Preliminary research indicates that the yield from agricultural crops can be reduced as a result of both the direct effects of acids on foliage and the indirect effects resulting from the leaching of minerals from soils. The productivity of forests may be similarly affected. In addition, acid deposition is contributing to the destruction of stone monuments and statuary throughout the world.

A report in the *New York Times* revealed that ozone, a major air pollutant, is costing the nation $2 billion to $4.5 billion a year in production losses on corn, wheat, soybeans, and peanuts.

In addition to crop damage and losses due to air and water pollution, agricultural productivity is also affected by soil erosion, loss of soil nutrients, compaction of soil, increasing salinization of both irrigated land and water used for irrigation, loss of high-quality cropland to urban development, extinction of local and wild crop strains needed by plant breeders for crop improvement, and water shortages.

Some of the other environmental consequences are
• water pollution from heavy application of pesticides and fertilizers;
• deforestation resulting in unstable water runoff which in turn leads both to silting of streams, reservoirs behind hydroelectric dams, and irrigation works, and also to the depletion of ground water;
• deterioration of air quality especially in urban areas;
• rising carbon dioxide concentrations in the air and the deterioration of stratospheric ozone layers.

Energy is used in the production and distribution of everything. Therefore, its impacts on environment should be carefully examined. Energy continues to mean oil, at least for the next ten to twenty years. We have a virtual consensus that oil is a fast disappearing resource. The impacts of nuclear power plants are different from those related to fossil fuel combustion, but no less serious. The high costs of nuclear power plants, the risk of radioactive conntamination due to reactor accidents (e.g., Three Mile Island), and the problem of satisfactory disposal of radioactive waste make nuclear power a doubtful source for our future energy needs.

Solar energy has a great potential economically and environmentally, but there seems to be some resistance to it from corporate energy interests, and it will be a while before it becomes widespread.

Our economy, based on private gain, has felt the need for exponential rates of growth to satisfy the demands of the capital owners. Competition also forces firms to maximize profits in order to survive. Each entrepreneur attempts to run the factory in the most efficient manner. What does one do with the waste products from the plant? The market leaves one with little choice. These waste products must be disposed of as cheaply as possible. The result of this arrangement is pollution in various forms. No doubt the products will be cheaper for the consumer, but the consumer pays for it indirectly by way of water treatment to make water suitable for drinking, treatment of lung cancer and other environmentally-induced diseases, and so on.

Economists once thought of air and water resources as "free goods" and not as a normal economic commodity. Therefore, in the past, the environment did not figure in their pricing calculations. We now see that there are real costs to using the air and water around us. Air and water can be depleted or degraded like any other resource.

Lester Brown of World Watch Institute describes pollution as "the generation of excessive waste." It is the overloading of the earth's built-in capacity to absorb waste. Nature has an amazing capacity to absorb waste (e.g., flowing streams), but that capacity is not unlimited. Pollution control, therefore, is now receiving the attention of certain large-scale enterprises.

A good example of an industry becoming involved in pollution control and making it profitable is found in the 3M Company. The company reduced 70,000 tons of noxious gas and 500 million tons of waste water. In the process, they saved $70 million per year.

Environmental protection has become a new business. It is also a job creator. The environmental business in the U.S. was worth about $50 billion in 1980 and has been increasing at the rate of about 20 percent per year. In terms of job creation, the U.S. Environmental Protection Agency commissioned a study for the period 1971-81 which has revealed that close to a million jobs were created by the requirements of environmental protection.

The environmental issue brings into sharp focus the debate of whether we should aim for a continuing growth economy or a steady-state economy. Both options have their supporters, but a large majority of economists and politicians seem to defend a growth economy. The advocates of a steady-state should be raising questions such as what is the minimum acceptable growth? What is the maximum? Is no-growth a viable option? Under what conditions, can a no-growth society provide employment for everyone? What would happen to the rising expectations of the disadvantaged in a slow-growing or no-growth society?

Those who advocate continued growth must ask, what good is a rising material standard of living if our natural environment is polluted beyond a safe level? Can we generate economic growth without using ever greater resource inputs?

Christendom's view of nature has been incomplete, perhaps lop-sided. Christians have a biblical mandate to develop a way of life which treats the whole creation with great care. Yet we are stuck with the environmental crisis because, for many years now, we have seen our destiny in terms of our conquest over nature: that is, we have seen the visible world as an enemy, a thing to be beaten down and then exploited. Experts have drawn our attention to the very serious dangers we are in. If we are to surmount the crisis, new techniques by themselves will not be enough. What we really need is repentance and a broadened understanding of the concept of stewardship of creation.

## II. Our Educational Systems

Since our schools and colleges are such an integral part of both our social and economic structure, let us review some aspects of our educational system. It is important for us to examine three major influences on the American educational system. They are the government, the military, and the private (business) sector.

Let us first examine the role of government in education. Keeping the common schools "above politics" was one of the concerns of those who shaped public education in the past. Public education from kindergarten through college has always been supported by strong political coalitions.

The federal government's involvement in both primary and secondary education, beginning about twenty-five years ago, was primarily linked to national defense. Spurred by Soviet space achievements, for example, Congress established the National Defense Student Loan program to stimulate college attendance, particularly in science and technology.

In the 1960s the focus began to shift to domestic concerns. President Johnson, who wanted to be remembered as the "Education President," was instrumental in raising the educational opportunities for the disadvantaged groups. Under his leadership, the federal government embarked on a program of full-scale aid to elementary and secondary schools and to students in institutions of higher education.

The vast investment of federal funds was initiated by President Johnson because it was perceived that better schooling was a remedy, in part, for the national problems that included security, poverty, economic growth, and racial inequality. The federal government assumed a role not only in funding but also in curriculum development. Along with federal funding, state funding for education reached new levels.

The 1970s brought in the ascendancy of many special interest groups, each trying to advance its own cause without much conscious concern for the overall welfare of national education. Schools were also influenced by this phenomenon, particularly by groups committed to the advancement of the handicapped and ethnic and racial minorities.

When the middle class began to identify the real impact of these programs—the creation of equity between the classes and races—enthusiasm for such expanded appropriations waned perceptibly. Public education became very controversial.

One important spin-off of federal involvement in education has been in the establishment of hundreds of privately supported schools. The origin of some of these institutions reflects racial prejudice as white families responded to busing requirements imposed upon public school children. Other schools are started by middle class parents, black and white, who feel that public schools are less attentive to the needs of their children. A question to consider is whether this is a healthy development in our society at this stage.

*Militarism in Public Education*

Let us now examine the impact of militarism on education. With the development of the atom bomb (1945), the fields of mathematics and science, associated with the success of the war effort, increased in importance. Academic accomplishment was considered crucial for national survival and so university education received an unprecedented boost. The GI Bill helped expand higher education enormously. This GI Bill, coupled with the focus on higher education, helped to emphasize the importance of education to the American people.

In October of 1957, *Sputnik I* produced a reaction which caused further reform of the American educational system. Suddenly, the U.S. defense felt threatened, and a vast national effort in education was deemed necessary. The seeds for militarism and the militarization of education had been planted, and the tree has kept growing bigger ever since that time.

Odd though it may appear, the Pentagon is still very much a part of the education-information structure of the United States. For more than three decades, the armed forces have been training millions of young men and acquiring useful information about the educational process. In 1968, Clark Clifford, then Secretary of Defense, observed, "The Department of Defense is one of the world's largest educators and should be one of the world's best. We train military people in 1500 separate skills, and our schools for service children are in 28 countries around the globe." The Pentagon has even moved into some of the functions which were previously reserved for civilian authorities. For example, the Domestic Action Program, which provides summer camps for disadvantaged ghetto youths, is run by the military. This and other programs run by the military blur the distinction between military and civilian sectors. These programs also help to gain public support for military programs.

The Defense Department's plans for exploring the role of the military in education and the transformation of higher education first unfolded in a speech by Thomas W. Carr, then Director of Defense Education, Office of the Secretary of Defense—Manpower, Reserve Affairs, and Logistics. In 1977, Carr argued, "By 1984 . . . the military will become a major instrument for youth socialization—assuming a large portion of the role once dominated by the family, the church, the school, and the civilian work setting."

Colleges and universities are affected by the same economic and demographic trends that affect the military. Costs are rising and the pool of young people from which to recruit is getting smaller. But, Carr observes, "The potential battle between the military and higher education will be avoided by simply joining together in a series of cooperative ventures. Approximately one-half million armed services people are already involved in various types of educational programs costing over $1 billion annually. Most of this education is provided by civilian institutions—over 1,000 of them at last count."

Mr. Carr talks about the "cooperative" character of the

ever-increasing "partnership" between the military and education. However, in view of the real possibility of empty classrooms and shrinking budgets, it is easy to see the opportunity for the military to become the dominant partner in this partnership. The new collaboration has gone beyond the traditional Reserve Officer Training Corps (ROTC) programs. The military plans to become a major purchaser of adult education programs. This could give it a correspondingly large voice in all areas of curriculum in which it invests.

As was previously stated, one of the major educational areas of concern for the U.S. military is that of science/technology. The National Science Foundation, established after World War II, is supposed to be the chief financial source for academic science research. However, the campus research and development grants received from the military are now three fourths the size of those grants received from the National Science Foundation. In addition, the amount received from the military appears to be on the increase.

For over four decades after the testing of the atom bomb, we continued to spend over half a billion dollars of basic research funds annually for defense-related research at American college and university campuses. The Applied Physics Lab at Johns Hopkins University plays a central role in nuclear weapons research. The research laboratories at Los Alamos and Livermore, affiliated with the University of California, are integral to the production of nuclear weapons. While the armed services concentrate their campus research on seeking knowledge that will eventually be applicable to weapons, the Defense Department supports research in virtually all fields of study. They feel that no field of research is irrelevant to their purposes.

The Department of Defense had a strong relationship to the university community up through the early 1960s, but the relationship had weakened during the Vietnam War period.

Now, according to the Berkeley Study Group, "The revitaliza-
tion of Pentagon ties to academia is forging ahead in several
directions: renewed direct and indirect funding of military
projects, enhanced long-term military-academic relationships
and interdependencies, and nurturance of a cadre of academic
consultants and special study groups."

*Business Interests in Education*

Let us finally examine the influence of the private
(business) sector on American education. An important shift in
the U.S. economy has taken place since World War II. Our
work force has been growing more rapidly in the service and information areas than in the goods manufacturing sector. By
some estimates, almost half of our work force, including
students, is presently associated with the "knowledge industry." Others have observed that the education industry is
second only to the defense industry in size. Both these observations must have some measure of truth in them. Why else
would private profit-seeking corporations and the military
establishment have mobilized themselves to harness public
education to their own interests and goals?

With expanded federal and state funding for education,
education became a growth industry. This attracted the
business community to the profits in the market for educational materials. A sweeping reorganization of the publishing
industry and their absorption by electronic corporations is a
dramatic example of the rush to make profits. As a result of all
these developments, the power for educational changes has
shifted from teachers colleges and superintendents' offices to
corporate offices and executive suites. Big business has decided that the "knowledge industry" will be profitable.

Historically, education has been a public responsibility.
Regardless of the nation's meager resources in the early years
of the Republic, this remained true. At a time of overwhelming
national affluence, it is ironic that education is in danger of

being turned over to the exploitation of private profit-seeking organizations. The educational sector of corporate capitalism is not so much interested in solving the deepening crisis in American education as in the potential profits this market affords it.

Educational institutions cannot compete with the salaries offered by corporations and the military contractors. Talented persons are drawn away from the field of education. Also, the federal presence in the classroom, although more controversial now than ever, is unlikely to diminish. Against the background of economic decline and political pressure, politicians will probably continue to make major decisions about the appropriate role for government in education. For those who subscribe to the belief that our youth represent the most important resource, the future of education looks dismal at best.

# 10
# Inflation and Unemployment

## I. Inflation

Inflation is a steady rise in prices. It is not some going up and others going down, but all or most going up together. Along with prices, wages and salaries tend to go up in an inflationary period. Inflation is one of our major economic problems.

Inflation is not a new phenomenon. What is new are the high rates of inflation experienced over the last fifteen years or so. Since 1967, there has been a rapid continuing rise in prices. Between January 1970 and late October 1979, prices exactly doubled. The rate of inflation during the 1970s averaged a little over seven percent annually—more than triple what it had averaged in the previous two decades. As the 1970s ended, inflation was well into double digits.

Depending on whom we ask, we get a variety of explanations of why we have inflation. The blame for inflation has been placed on labor leaders, corporate executives, farmers, consumers, federal budget deficits, high interest rates, federal spending on social welfare, high Pentagon budgets, OPEC or "The Arabs" and the seven major oil companies, the money supply controlled by the Federal Reserve System, the banks, Presidents past and present, the Soviet grain deal and the companies who sold the grain, government regulations, and many other factors like minimum wage laws, speculation, and so on. But what is really responsible for inflation?

It is difficult to single out any one of these commonly mentioned causes as the one responsible for inflation. Some of the factors have played a more significant role than others, while some have had no effect on inflation. However, we can identify several elements that contribute to the problem of inflation.

One such element is that a predisposition to inflation is built into the fundamental structure of our economy. This is true for the simple reason that when the price of a commodity goes up, inflation automatically occurs, unless other prices and incomes fall proportionately. However, prices and wages in other sectors do not easily fall, and inflation continues.

In our democratic set-up we organize to protect our economic interest, and our success inevitably leads to inflation. Everyone wants more. As a result both prices and wages tend to move upward. Employers, especially if they are big enough, find it easier to pay higher wages and then raise prices than to risk a strike. Legislators find it easier to approve new programs or increase subsidy levels than to take unpopular measures.

A second element is found in government spending. Government spending plays an enormous part in our modern economy. For example, the federal government pours billions of dollars into the economy for military-related procurements. Similarly, because of its huge size, the government can stimulate economic activity and take other measures to smooth out the business cycle and prevent depressions. In a recession, the government usually pumps money into the economy and gives tax cuts so consumers can spend more money. This assists the sluggish economy to pick up momentum. And most voters approve of such governmental actions. The government also has the option to adopt policies to slow down inflation. But unlike the policies used to fight a depression, policies to curb inflation involve higher taxation, higher interest rates, and so on. These measures take money away from consumers. Most politicians, naturally, prefer to shy away from such unpopular measures. This poses a systemic dilemma which makes our economy predisposed to a continuing inflation.

### Consequences of Inflation

Is inflation making us poorer? Has it resulted in a decline of the real standard of living? Although prices doubled in the 1970s, most Americans were making more than twice as much at the end of the decade as they had been at the beginning. Therefore, the purchasing power of most families has kept upward. While some people have suffered, in general, the poor are not poorer nor the rich richer. Some goods and services are relatively cheaper than they used to be, some relatively more expensive. In a growing economy, usually, incomes rise faster than prices.

Economists tell us that most Americans have experienced a real income (i.e., income adjusted for inflation) gain of 15 percent from 1972 to 1978. Why then do most people say they have been hurt by inflation? The money income is rising maybe at four to five times the rate at which the real income has been rising. This being the case, economists explain, people feel that inflation is taking away what is rightfully their own while forgetting that inflation raised the money income in the first place.

Inflation does not affect everyone equally. Some people suffer from inflation, others actually profit from it. Who are the winners and losers? The income of some groups—police officers, physicians, and construction workers—have almost exactly matched the rise in prices. Other groups, such as unionized factory workers and truck drivers, have managed to raise their incomes substantially faster than inflation. Steelworkers' pay went up 165 percent; auto workers', 146 percent; and truckers', 122 percent. The elderly have more than kept pace primarily because of the social security system which accounts for roughly half of all the income going to them. Private pensions too have helped the elderly a great deal.

On the average, employees in retail trade, finance, insurance, and real estate lost ground. College professors, librarians, certain categories of salespersons, domestic servants, and free-lance writers did not do well either. Welfare recipients, single-parent families, and workers on minimum wage did badly.

As expected, the lowest income groups suffer more than other income groups. And since the low income groups include women and minorities, they are the ones who are hurt the most by inflation. Welfare recipients, for example, under the Aid to Families with Dependent Children (AFDC) program had an inflationary loss of about 20 percent in real income between 1970 and 1978.

Even though the real income of some poor people has kept pace with inflation, the poor are hurt whenever the cost of basic necessities, such as food, housing, and heat, rises faster than overall inflation. The poor can least afford these increases because their disposable income is less "disposable." A higher proportion of it was already going to such expenses, leaving less surplus to absorb the increases. Low cost, rent-controlled housing becomes less available as landlords, not entitled to raise rents, convert their apartment buildings into condominiums or abandon them.

Inflation combined with slow economic growth reduces the size of the overall economic pie and when that happens, the people on low fixed income get a decreased share of jobs and new social programs.

Inflation also weakens the quality of education in the public schools, the educational system on which the poor depend almost entirely. This comes about as middle class parents, dissatisfied with poor quality education, transfer their children to private schools. Once that takes place, they are less likely to vote for higher school taxes. The poor, for whom private schools are not an option, are stuck with low quality education for their children and subsequently with lost opportunity for bettering their children's future.

Can our society accept inflation as something that is desirable and ignore it as a problem? Inflation cannot be ignored because it perpetuates uncertainty. Under a continuing inflation, the ordinary uncertainties of an individual's income and wealth are heightened a great deal. Inflation also directly hits a much larger number of people than does unemployment. Moreover, inflation may be among the causes of unemployment. As both unemployment and inflation are grave social ills plaguing our economy, they must receive serious attention.

Inflation presents a dilemma to government policy makers both economically and politically. One method of controlling inflation is with recession. This we have experienced since 1980. A second method of controlling inflation is through formal wage and price control. Such controls are supplemented with a variety of other measures like rationing (e.g., energy), holding the line on wages and benefits for government employees, and so on. Both of these policy options have drawbacks and, seemingly, are difficult to implement. However, some comprehensive system of control, short of asking the government to actually run the economy, is about the only anti-inflationary program that is potentially feasible and effective in our type of economy. Even controls cannot succeed without the private and public sectors of the economy doing their part seriously.

Governmental intervention is not such a radical step because the government is deep into the economy now, and it is logical for it to take all necessary steps in an effort to stabilize the economy for the good of all. Whether an economy-wide governmental intervention will ever happen or not remains an open question.

## II. UNEMPLOYMENT

Calvin Coolidge defined unemployment simply, "When a great

many people are out of work, unemployment results." Full
employment is defined in the U.S. in terms of the rate of
unemployment. This has varied from one administration to
another over the past two decades. When John Kennedy
became President, "full employment" was said to be achieved
when only three percent of the work force were unemployed.
Under Lyndon Johnson it became four percent; under Richard
Nixon and Gerald Ford it became five percent; under Jimmy
Carter it headed toward six percent. Today, for most
economists, full employment means seven percent unemployment. In terms of numbers it means that if only seven million
Americans are without work we still have "full employment."
Statistics are necessary for us to understand what is happening in our society. Yet, numbers do not tell the whole story,
and we have to grasp the assumptions underlying the numbers
in order to get a true picture of reality.

There are two root causes of unemployment in our
economy: the business cycle and technological innovation.

Capitalism is cyclical, i.e., it survives alternating periods of
boom-and-bust, prosperity and recession. The business cycle results in plant closings, layoffs, and unemployment. When products do not sell, workers lose jobs. The cycle itself is created mainly by the basic unplanned character of the economy. When there is
no coordination, business expansions take place independently
from what is happening in the overall economy. Recession helps
eliminate some producers, and the cycle begins again. The
economy seems unable to avoid or overcome this process.

Secondly, mechanization and automation also contribute
to unemployment. The basic motivation is the bottom line, or
profits. And the easiest way to increase profits is to cut costs.
Labor is the place where the costs are the easiest to reduce, and
machines help to accomplish that goal.

*Controlling Unemployment*
Four policies are used in our economy to deal with

unemployment. First are the federal government's efforts to smooth out the business cycle. When in a recession, give the economy a boost; when the economy is overheated,[1] slow it down. These efforts take the form of manipulations of the money supply or interest rates or of tax cuts and spending programs. These methods are generally well-known because they are the kind of economic policy that is most publicized.

The problem is that these remedial measures require continual governmental intervention and stimulation to keep them going. Besides, they are becoming less and less effective.

The second method of dealing with the business cycle is by some form of planning. The U.S. is one of the least planned of the major capitalist economies. The governments of England, France, West Germany, and Japan are greatly involved in economic planning. Sometimes, this planning takes the form of providing voluntary targets for businesses to adopt. Other times, it involves more direct involvement in the economy with government actually planning investment programs. This approach is used in Japan, where government and business are sometimes difficult to distinguish from one another. The important question is, who is going to do the planning and in whose interest is the planning to be done?

The third policy addresses the long-term tendency to produce fewer and fewer jobs, a tendency attributable to technology. It is thought that by encouraging faster economic growth, more jobs will be available. This policy, however, can have serious detrimental effects on the environment. From a capitalist's perspective, unemployment is not necessarily a bad thing; it provides a ready source of labor, and it helps keep down wages. Hence, a policy of rapid economic growth appears attractive in the short run. But if rising wages begin to cut into profits, that same capitalist may help precipitate a recession anyway by cutting back on investment.

To use economic growth as a way of dealing with the unemployment is, therefore, a very uncertain policy from both the capitalist perspective and the perspective of people outside of the corporations.

The fourth policy is *public employment*. This has been relied upon only in periods of severe recession. We saw it in a fairly large scale in the New Deal. Now and then, there is still talk about public employment as a means of dealing with unemployment.

This policy has problems too. The basic problem is that a public employment program has to be paid for out of tax dollars. People are very hesitant to let their tax dollars be used in this way because they feel that money for these projects comes out of their pockets. With the kind of massive unemployment we have today and the general public's resistance to public employment programs, this approach holds little promise.

### Inflation and Unemployment

There is also a possible correlation between inflation and unemployment. In the attempt to control inflation with a recession, layoffs are increased. It is a case of creating one problem to solve another. Inflation, therefore, can be considered a cause of unemployment. For example, in 1982 the double-digit inflation rate of the 1970s was brought down to 3.9 percent; unemployment, however, rose significantly from 5.8 percent in 1979 to 10.8 percent in December 1982.

If a recession helps bring down the rate of inflation, are the costs worth it? According to the late economist Arthur Okun, 90 percent of the effect of a prolonged recession is lost output and jobs, and only 10 percent is diminished inflation. The human costs of unemployment resulting from a recession are too high, not to mention the idle plant operations and business failures which also result.

The costs of unemployment are twofold. There is loss of output, or production, and loss of morale for those experiencing unemployment.

A continuing high level of unemployment lowers the quality of life by heightening uncertainty, sharpening social conflict, and creating hostility toward the economic and political institutions that are thought to be responsible for it.

The burden of unemployment usually falls heavily on people who weren't doing so well to begin with. The burden is borne disproportionately by black and Hispanic workers, by female workers, and by the young. In the 1982 recession the unemployment rate for blacks was 18.7 percent in May (49.8 percent for black teenagers) as compared to the overall rate of 9.5 percent for all workers.

Unemployment, like inflation, is endemic to our economy. Politically, the prospects of solving the problem of unemployment are not good. This is true mainly because of the way the labor force is divided in our industrial capitalism. Our working class can be divided into two segments. A tenured segment consists of those with a considerable degree of job security. The nontenured segment receives low wages, has irregular employment, has little job security and gains little benefit from greater seniority or education.

The tenured segment is secure and worries little about the possibility of personal unemployment, except during a deep recession. This segment forms an influential, steadily growing component of the voting population. Their prime concern is inflation, and political realism draws the politicians to their side. The nontenured are a substantial minority, but they still lack political clout. Therefore, unemployment is less likely to receive adequate attention as long as inflation exists on the political agenda. And inflation will remain an issue for a long time to come.

The challenge lies in devising methods of stopping inflation without creating high unemployment, a far more serious problem than inflation.

In December 1982, at an unemployment rate of 10.8 percent, 12 million American workers had no jobs. This is the highest level of unemployment in 40 years. If the number of "discouraged workers" (those who say they have given up seeking employment) were added to the total unemployed, the jobless rate would reach 12.5 percent. In addition to the 12 million who were looking for work, about 5.8 million were employed only part-time.

A growing jobless rate influences federal deficits. The budget makers figure that each rise of a percentage point in the jobless rate sustained over a year costs $20 billion to $30 billion in outlays for unemployment insurance payments. When these unanticipated outlays are combined with the loss of taxes that would have been paid by those who lost their jobs, the impact on the federal budget is substantial.

The ranks of the jobless are growing at a time when many of the programs aimed at softening the pains of unemployment are being curtailed. This fact alone cannot help but direct people's attention to the seriousness of unemployment as an issue. In December 1981 only 36 percent of the 9.5 million jobless received unemployment compensation as compared to more than 75 percent of the 8.4 million jobless Americans who received benefits at the height of the 1973-75 recession. The question is, how are the remaining 63 percent of the unemployed going to support themselves and their families? Christians are called to be on the side of the poor and the dispossessed. A deep question for Christians is, can our economic system survive without inflation and unemployment?

# 11
# Impacts of
# the Economy

Under the impact of our economic system, certain kinds of problems tend to develop. Since these problems are not experienced equally by all persons, they are sometimes overlooked. This chapter suggests several of the specific problems which seem to be inherent in our economy.

*Poverty in America*

The word *poverty* seems to have a stigma in the American society. It is not uncommon to describe the poor with such euphemisms as the "culturally deprived," the "underprivileged," the "disadvantaged," the "low-income" groups, or the "other America." The latest vogue word used by the media is the "underclass," which includes the poor, the homeless, the welfare recipients, and the street criminals. The response to poverty varies with the person's worldview as well as political leanings. And so we find that conservatives deplore poverty and hope it will go away; the reactionaries blame the victims, taking no personal responsibility to change the society; the progressives get angry and blame "the system"; the "other worldly" idealize poverty and consider it virtuous.

Who are the poor? Since the biggest single group in our labor force is white, the white people are a large group in the working poor category. We also have the racial minorities (Afro-Americans, Mexican-Americans, Puerto Ricans, Native Americans), unemployed workers, migrant laborers, small farmers, women who are heads of households, employees in low-wage industries, the unskilled, the mentally ill, and many others.

The poor could be called the outcasts and the untouchables of American society because they are left out of the main-stream of the society. Their poverty is perhaps not as un-bearable as the disabilities they suffer because of such social stigmas as color, ethnic origin, religion, old age, mental illness, or lack of technical skills. They become the rejects of a technocratic capitalism that has made them redundant in the productive process. They receive low social esteem and are ascribed a social and political status of vulnerability and powerlessness. They lack any effective power to assert their wishes and needs.

Our economic system is concerned with the production and exchange of goods and services for the purpose of pro-viding profits to owners and investors of capital. The economy, as such, is not concerned with poverty. It has no reason to focus on alleviation of the poverty or the problems of the poor. Are poverty and inequality necessary byproducts for capital-ism to function as a system, or are they defects which can be remedied some way? Economists differ in viewpoints on these questions.

Some economists would say that poverty and inequality are inherent to capitalism. By this they mean that the institu-tions which define the capitalist system cannot function prop-erly without producing poverty and inequity. To say it dif-ferently, they argue that some poverty and inequality are necessary to the system of incentives and control within the private economy.

Excessive poverty could lead to pressure for significant social change. However, some poverty is economically benefi-cial in the long run, as long as it can be accommodated without reaching the point of social disruption.

What role do poverty and inequality play in our economy?

First, extreme wage and income inequality seem necessary to induce workers to perform work for monetary reward rather than for job satisfaction. Second, the poor class is used as a warning to the nonpoor to stay in line lest their own fate get worse. Third, the poor help keep wages down, unions weak, and labor's bargaining power low in so far as the poor serve as a reserve pool of the unemployed. Finally, we, the nonpoor, benefit from the existence of poverty because commodities and services are available to us at lower prices, and that increases our real income substantially.

By way of contrast to the above viewpoint, the orthodox economists view poverty as the result of the failure of the individual to acquire the necessary skills in order to find employment. It places the responsibility on the individual rather than on the system within which the individual has to perform. Usually our response to poverty depends upon which of these two analyses makes more sense to us.

*Fighting Poverty*

The economic system does not have a way to deal with the poor. Yet, poverty cannot be ignored by a society that insists upon the worth of all its citizens and equality of their political and social rights. Therefore, the *society* has to deal with the problems of the poor. That is, our government and other social institutions must respond to poverty in lieu of the economic system. The real dilemma we face is that our political and social institutions are not in *direct* control of what the poor need most, namely, a place in the economic reward system. Therefore, under the present situation, the response of our government and other social institutions is indirect and mainly through three types of activity.

• Help to meet the immediate basic survival needs of the poor, both for those who are without incomes (the unemployed) and for those whose incomes are not enough to meet the basic needs (the underemployed)—welfare, food

stamps, other forms of aid, and public service jobs.
• Help to prepare those who are poor to become more attractive to the economy, which can then admit them to participation and reward them—education and training, etc.
• Help to provide incentives for the private economy to include the poor—affirmative action, government procurement policies, Project Equality, subsidized private sector jobs, etc.

For nearly a century, the federal government stayed out of the arena of deprivation and misery. Then it began to intervene systematically to correct major areas of economic deprivation.

The government has taken action to provide to the poor services like moderate-cost housing, health care, and urban transportation, which are not available from the private sector or in which the private economy defaults. Government has adopted measures to protect people from circumstances with which they cannot, as an individual, contend. These are measures for smoothing and softening the harsh edges of capitalism. However, the trend seems to be in the direction of reducing social programs for the poor and using public resources to stimulate the private economy. It has also been suggested that private philanthropy and volunteerism should now play a major role to assist the poor. Professor James Tobin of Yale writes, "The U.S. budget and tax legislation of 1981 is an historic reversal of direction. The message is clear enough: inequality of opportunity is no longer a concern of federal government." In view of that trend it becomes doubly important for Christians to monitor closely our government's social policy and programs, particularly in so far as they have impact on the poor and needy. What are the "social programs" of the federal government?

The Federal government operates two types of "social programs": those which are available to all persons regardless of their income level and those which are restricted to persons with low incomes. Programs in the first group provide most of their benefits and services to persons who have incomes above the poverty line. This group includes Social Security, Medicare, civil service retirement and military retirement. These programs comprise the vast bulk of all federal spending for social programs.

The basic support programs for the low-income persons include Aid to Families with Dependent Children (AFDC—the basic welfare program for poor families); food stamps; Medicaid (as opposed to Medicare); Supplemental Security Income for the aged and disabled poor; free school meals; low income energy assistance; low-income housing; compensatory education for low-income children; employment and training for the poor and unskilled; legal services; food supplements for poor pregnant women, infants, and children; and other social services for homebound elderly persons.

A popular view among much of the American public is that these "welfare type" programs consume huge proportions of the federal budget. The realities, however, are that 14 percent of the population is still below the poverty level and that the combined cost of welfare and food stamps represents about 10 percent of the budget. Contrary to much talk about the uncontrolled costs of welfare and food stamps, the largest share of budget dollars simply does not go to programs for the poor. Expenditures for Social Security, Medicare, and the other retirement programs are three times larger than the cost of *all* the low-income programs. In dollar figures, the 1982 federal outlays for AFDC were about $8 billion; for food stamps about $11.5 billion; in contrast, the military retirement program alone was $15 billion; civil service retirement nearly $20 billion, and Medicare about $50 billion.

Some budget-watchers on Capitol Hill expect a reduction of more than 45 percent in real dollars (i.e., dollars adjusted for inflation) from about $100 billion in fiscal 1981.

*Economy and Racism*

The economic effects of racism in the U.S. include differentials in income, occupational status, health standards, and quality of life in general. The median black incomes have been fluctuating between 47 percent and 63 percent of median white incomes with the ratio rising during economic expansions and falling to previous low levels during recessions. In virtually every field, black earnings are less than white earnings in the same jobs.

In the occupational status as well, whites have maintained a relative advantage over people of color. The unemployment rate of blacks regularly runs at least double that of whites. Between one third and one half of all black teenage job-seekers cannot find work.

Technological innovation including mechanization of the harvest during the 1950s eliminated most poor blacks from agricultural employment and forced them to move to larger cities for economic survival. By 1980, 81.3 percent of the black population was located in urban centers and concentrated in racial ghettos. When blacks moved from the rural South to urban centers, instead of finding liberation from racism they found racism in new forms. Although they migrated from the South toward areas of higher wages and narrower racial income differentials, still the gap between black and white incomes is quite remarkable. Why is this so?

Many would attribute the continuing income inequality to the incorporation of blacks into the urban working class in ways that reproduced rather than eliminated racism. Instead of a national mobilization to correct the basic problem of their being "left behind by technology"—for example, an educational program that would prepare them for absorption into the mainstream economy—they were treated as a new social problem. A social policy of welfare at subsistence level (or lower) and some transfer payment in kind, like food stamps, were formulated in the hope that with the break in the inflationary cycle, the blacks would find employment.

Besides blacks, the other racial minorities in the United States—Chicanos, Puerto Ricans, American Indians, Asian Americans—also experience racism. Racial factors thus continue to be prominent in American workers' lives.

Does racism help the cause of capitalism? Some say racism is an aberration in the U.S. which will gradually disappear in a democratic capitalist society. But there are others who see racism as useful, though not necessary, for capitalism to function as an economic system. They argue that capitalism nurtures racist practices and ideologies which help to stabilize its position and gain for itself the profit-making advantage it always seeks. How can capitalism achieve stability through racism? The division of the working class based on racial and sexual discrimination creates a surplus labor force which can serve several functions. First of all, it can be employed at lower wage rates. Secondly the visible differences of race and sex can be played upon in creating divisions among workers. Historically, for example, race has been used during crisis periods, and black strike-breakers have been imported by employers to stir racial hatred and undermine strike solidarity.

Racism helps capitalism in noneconomic ways as well. For its own stability, capitalism has to devise ways to legitimize the system, and racism is one way to legitimize inequality, alienation, and powerlessness. For example, many whites believe that welfare payments to blacks are a far more important factor in their taxes than is military spending. Through racism, poor whites come to believe that their poverty is caused by blacks who are willing to take away their jobs at lower wages. This conceals the fact that a substantial amount of inequality is inevitable in the capitalist society. Racism thus serves the purpose of transferring white resentment for their plight to blacks and away from the system.

*Sex and the Economy*

In the last twenty years, the efforts of the feminist movement have brought to light the patterns and incidences of sexism experienced by women in the United States. Sexism (or male dominance) is much in evidence in the economic arena in the reality that women do not have the same economic opportunities as men and that women still have the primary responsibility for parenting and for housework, whether or not they hold a paying job.

Although the patriarchal family pattern of old times is no longer in existence, the result has not been equality for women. Instead, a system of inequality has evolved, firmly rooted in the needs of the capitalistic economic system. The contemporary American family is generally male dominant and embodies sexual inequalities. Capitalism undermined patriarchy, but male dominance has survived and continues to the benefit of the economic system. What functions could a male-dominant family perform for capitalism?

In a male-dominant family, a crucial function is provided by the women. The emotional work of women in the areas of interpersonal relationships and in the emotional development and support for children and men enables the family to function in a capitalist society. This emotional stability becomes doubly important in an advanced capitalist society like the U.S.

As discussed earlier, sexism is carried over into the labor market, which segregates jobs unequally by sex. The practice of sexism is very useful for capital owners who employ women as wage workers. It gives employers an exploitable labor surplus made up of women who lack the economic support of a husband and of women who want temporary work. And as pointed out earlier, such subordinated women provide a convenient cushion, or a reserve labor force, which can be used when business is booming and released during downswings. Many of the least-paid jobs in the economy are filled by women in this category of reserve labor.

Women play a significant role in the U.S. economy. They have always contributed to the nation's economy, but never before have women of America played a more important role in the economic security of the family and the economic growth of the country. The consumer economy depends on women and so does the productive economy. Women handle the money that runs the economy, yet only a fraction of that money ends up in their pocketbooks. Capitalism could not survive without women supporting the male workers or, at home, without women as consumers and as low-paid workers. The emphasis has been on a full-time home worker role for women and on women as consumers of commodities.

When we look at the place of women in the U.S. economy, three striking themes stand out. First, there has been an enormous increase in the number and proportion of women who work outside the home. Although women had begun to enter the labor force from the beginning of the Industrial Revolution, by 1980 they had come to make up 43 percent of it.

Second, occupations and jobs tend to be separated by gender, and the degree of such segregation has not diminished over the years. Managerial, professional, and other skilled positions are often denied to women.

Third, the increase of women in the labor force has been accompanied by a widening income differential between men and women, with women continuing to receive lower pay than men. Despite the Equal Pay Act (1963), the average woman worker today makes 59 cents to every dollar a man makes. The average wage for a woman worker is under $9,000 a year.

### Social Hazards of the Economy

The impact which our economy has on individuals can be seen in the way the system deals with persons in those situations which arise specifically as a result of their being involved as workers within the economic system. James E. Vermeulen, a former asbestos worker, is now executive director of

Asbestos Victims of America.

Speaking on industrial safety and injury compensation before the House Subcommittee on Commerce, Transportation and Tourism, March 16, 1982, he said:

> When I went to work for industry, I just knew that they, like my parents would never knowingly let me do anything that would harm me. I felt that if I worked hard and applied myself I would be rewarded and protected. Personally I feel it would have been more merciful for me to have been killed in action while defending our nation than to die this lingering death inflicted upon me by an industry whose right to operate and make money I helped to preserve.
>
> In 1977 my American dream turned into a nightmare when the time bomb of abestos exploded within my chest. My working career completely ended at that time. I was transformed from a hard-working, proud individual to a nothing. The gloom and depression that settled upon me led to the brink of suicide.
>
> My wife and I learned that I breathed much better on the coast near the ocean. I didn't have to use my portable oxygen unit quite so much there. We moved, leaving our family, friends and loved ones behind, to a totally strange area in the hopes that we would buy me a little more time for living.
>
> We were forced to pay over $11,000 in medical bills because the insurance companies had cut me off, saying it was an occupational injury. I didn't qualify for Medicare because my disease was occupationally caused. Our compensation systems throughout our state and nation are nothing more than a sad, sick joke.
>
> We have an asbestos disease epidemic. Our workplaces need inspection and supervision to prevent the companies from slipping back into their lethal practices before OSHA.
>
> Dying is a tough way to make a living.

Mr. Vermeulen's case is neither isolated nor unique nor exceptional. Many workers meet with similar experiences in a variety of industrial situations and face occupational hazards in their jobs.

Plant shutdowns, corporate relocations, and capital mobility, that is, shifting a corporation's net productive capacity to another location (frequently outside of the U.S.) or putting that capital to other uses, are very common in our economy. Such corporate decisions, generally based on gaining larger profits, result in loss of jobs for thousands of workers. Workers are not consulted; often they are not informed of what is about to happen. It has been estimated that between 1969 and 1976 at least 15 million jobs were destroyed in the U.S. as a result of plant closings, an average of 2.1 million jobs per year.

What effect do these changes have on families and communities? Dr. M. Harry Brenner of Johns Hopkins University studied the "social trauma" caused by unemployment, and from his study he presented the following startling statistics to the Joint Economic Committee of the Congress in 1976. When unemployment rises one percentage point, 4.3 percent more men and 2.3 percent more women are admitted to state mental hospitals for the first time; 4.1 percent more people commit suicide; 5.7 percent more are murdered; four percent more people wind up in state prisons; and over a six-year period, 1.9 percent more people die from heart disease, cirrhosis of the liver, and other stress-related chronic ailments. Dr. Brenner estimated that the economic slump of 1970, with its 1.4 percent rise in unemployment, was linked to 51,570 additional deaths by 1975.

Plant closings create many social costs. They deprive people of the structure by which they hold their communities together. Plant closings also have a "ripple" effect on other employment. When steel mills shut down in Youngstown, for example, a recent study estimated the additional loss in jobs at 11,199, more than double the jobs lost in the steel shutdown itself.

Public policy related to plant closings and capital mobility in the U.S. are inadequate, to say the least. Existing policies tend to treat the effects rather than the causes of these problems. What is needed are appropriate public policies that would not only minimize the adverse impacts of the problems but also prevent their occurrence from becoming a common phenomenon.

Private ownership of the means of production is the principle on which our economy operates. Ownership bestows power and control to owners but places the worker in a vulnerable position. When we had a growing, expanding economy, the workers had room to bargain for their rights. However, in an economy that is shifting its locations and is perhaps sinking and stagnating, the lack of the power to participate in company decisions has become fatal for millions of workers This is evidenced by the rising unemployment. Therefore, the basic question arises, When workers are used to generate profit and capital which they can never own, is it morally right to manipulate that capital in such a manner that it destroys the workplace on which those workers' livelihoods depend and from which the security of the workers' families and community grows?

# 12
# U.S. Economy and Global Economy

This chapter is a conversation between Robert (Bob) Scott, an Anglican priest from New Zealand who worked for a time at the United Nations as an observer of global negotiations for the nongovernmental organizations at the U.N., and Shantilal Bhagat, Church of the Brethren staff member for Global Justice and United Nations representative.

**Bob:** Looking at the United States as a non-American, I view it as the most powerful and wealthy economy in the world. Why has it been that, in a comparatively short historical time, the United States' economy has become the most powerful and the most wealthy?

**Shantilal:** I can think of at least three reasons. First, the economic supremacy of the U.S. has been based on a land rich in mineral, energy, and climatic resources. No other country "inherited" more wealth than the United States. Secondly, there is the resourcefulness of the people who settled the land and saw the need to mechanize due to a shortage of labor. This led to a rapid expansion of the economy.

The third reason has to do with the nature of the capitalistic economic system adopted by the United States. One characteristic of capitalism is to seek a continuous growth in order to survive. Once the domestic U.S. economy was well developed, the capital owners looked for expansion outside the U.S.

**Bob:** When did U.S. capitalism recognize its need to internationalize the economy in order to support continuous, sustained growth in the U.S.?

**Shantilal:** I do not know if one can fix the exact time when the
economy felt the need to internationalize, but the full flowering
of multinational operations occurred only after World War II.
The U.S. was the only industrialized country which emerged
unscathed from the ravages of the war. U.S. industries, which
were geared up for a high rate of wartime production, were left
intact and the U.S. did not hesitate to use its advantageous
position in the world. Multinational operations bring a higher
profit rate. For example, in 1980 U.S. multinationals got a
return of 45.2 percent in Asia, 39.8 percent in Africa, and 19.4
percent in Latin America as compared to about 10 percent on
investments at home.

**Bob:** There is a suggestion by some historians that there was,
in fact, a plan by the United States to take advantage of
postwar failed economics. Is there any truth to this claim?

**Shantilal:** During World War II, the State Department planners and the Council of Foreign Relations met for a period of
six years (1939-45) in the War and Peace Studies Program.
They came up with a Grand Area Planning concept defining
the Grand Area as the area "strategically necessary for world
control." They also came to a determination that for the U.S.
economy to prosper, it would be necessary to have under its
control, at the minimum, the entire western hemisphere, the
former British Empire, and the Far East.

**Bob:** I don't see that as malicious. It is perfectly legitimate for
a country to want to internationalize its economy in order to
sustain its own growth. Unfortunately, there have been some
consequences of that expansion, and I am not at all sure we

fully understand what the consequences are.

**Shantilal:** One of the obvious consequences of the global expansion is that technology is introduced into the developing countries with no regard paid to the needs of the people or the specific situation of the country concerned. Only the need to make profits on investments receives attention. Therefore, the world develops, or industrializes, not according to the exercise of reason or foresight, but mainly to the dictates of self-expanding capital. For example, it is not uncommon to see highly automated industries exported into countries which have a surplus of labor. For a balanced development, these countries need industries which are labor-intensive rather than capital-intensive.

Technology does not operate in a vacuum. It is always at the service of some ideology or other. Technological development today has served the "ideology of consumerism." Under the pressure of consumerism, even "development" has been defined and measured in terms of increased Gross National Product or per capita income, and not in terms of liquidation of poverty and of distributive justice.

So we have a world which is continuously in a state of imbalance; there is monetary imbalance, trade imbalance, (that is, more imports than exports), resource imbalance (some countries have more resources than others), and finally there is developmental imbalance.

**Bob:** It strikes me that one never hears anyone disagreeing with what you have just said—that there are enormous imbalances in the world; that the international economy is in a state of disequilibrium; that there are few powerful economies and many powerless economies; that the majority of the economies in the world are weak. I think that the United States plays a very powerful role in that imbalance.

**Shantilal:** There is no question but that the United States is a very powerful force in the world economy.

While the U.S. plays a powerful role in the imbalances we spoke of, I think that the imbalances are likely to continue as long as the economic development of the world is left to the stimulus of private profit and private accumulation, without provision for mechanisms which can effectively or adequately allocate resources according to social needs.

Japan is one of the few countries which has effectively used state policies to care for some of the inadequacies of the market place. Corporate policy in Japan tends to stress long-range goals. I get the impression that the capitalist countries in general do not believe that it is in their economic interests to give in to the demands of the less developed countries, although I must admit there are some exceptions to this rule.

The socialist countries are also a part of the world capitalist market. Many of them have their own problems of low productivity, debts, and so forth, but they too, with some notable exceptions, have not shown active interest in the needs of the developing countries. What are your observations at the United Nations in this regard?

**Bob:** I see a number of countries (and I must say I would not number the United States among them) taking a longer term view than they did even five or ten years ago. They recognize that there is a very definite interdependence between developed and developing countries. The Scandinavian countries recognize it very clearly. This is evident in the speech of the representative of Sweden to the 36th General Assembly of the United Nations. There he said that development cooperation is a matter of survival, not of charity, and that the North in the wider perspective is just as dependent on the South as the South is on the North. The U.S. needs the markets of the developing countries who now purchase over 40% of U.S. manufactured exports. One out of every eight jobs in the United States comes from trade with developing countries.

The other side of the coin is that the U.S. absorbs about one-half of all manufactured goods that non-OPEC developing countries export to the industrialized world. There is no doubt a growing interdependence.

Within the last five or ten years, some countries have become aware that if they want to keep their own economies stable, they need to have markets. It is best to build those markets in countries with stable economies. Therefore, there is a long-term self-interest in helping to stabilize economies which up to now have been fragile.

**Shantilal:** What you just said brings to mind how interrelated the domestic economic policy decisions and foreign policy decisions are. It seems to me, for example, that the U.S. strategies in Central America are working at cross purposes. On the one hand, the administration has an economic plan for stimulating business in this area. On the other hand, its confrontational diplomacy threatens investor confidence.

Political instability is causing private investors, nationals and foreigners, to take capital out of Central America. Frightened Central American businessmen are moving their savings to Florida's banks and into the condominium market. The U.S. banks are also withdrawing money and corporate investments have come to a standstill. The World Bank stopped approving loans for El Salvador.

U.S. military strategy in Nicaragua and U.S. pursuit of military advances in El Salvador can only exacerbate investor uncertainty and economic decline. The U.S. policies in Central America raise the question of the rights of self-determination for the peoples of this region. It seems the U.S. sees its role mainly in military terms and/or economic terms without adequate consideration to human rights, including the right to self-determination. It is strange that the United States, which fought its own war of liberation from British colonial rule and has developed the concepts of democracy and freedom for its own people, should narrow its vision. This has the appearance of a double standard, and that is exactly how many of the developing countries view U.S. policies.

**Bob:** You referred to the effect of domestic economic policy on the global economy. How do you see that happening?

**Shantilal:** The U.S. dollar is international currency and is very important for international trade. There is, therefore, considerable pressure from U.S. trading partners i.e., the Economic Community (EEC), to maintain a stable dollar. So when President Reagan presented his projected 1983 budget with a huge deficit, the EEC immediately expressed concern that the deficit would keep interest rates high and intensify Europe's economic difficulties. They even sent a representative to talk things over with the Reagan administration.

High American interest rates cause the dollar to rise in value, and that affects Europe in two ways. European governments have to keep their own interest rates high to prevent large transfers of money into high-yielding, dollar-dominated investments. Secondly, Europe's oil bills rise because their oil imports are priced in dollars.

Expressing a grave concern about the deficits in Reagan's proposed 1983 budget and high interest rates, Chancellor Helmut Schmidt of West Germany said that they would contribute to a deep recession in Europe. Referring to high U.S. interest rates he said, "Right now the richest economy in the world is at the same time the greatest importer of capital." This is an unhealthy state. It is impossible to avoid the ripple effects of U.S. economic policies in the world.

**Bob:** Where do foreign aid and food aid fit into the global economic picture?

**Shantilal:** There are two schools of thought regarding the impact of aid on the developing countries. Some give unqualified support to foreign aid. They believe aid is always beneficial for the recipient nation and that without such aid the developing countries have little chance for economic growth. Others view foreign aid with a great deal of skepticism, believing that aid creates dependency and is harmful to the long-term interests of the recipients.

An obvious question is, how can aid be harmful? Military aid is harmful because in many countries it has helped to keep dictators in power who suppress their people and adopt policies which benefit only a few while keeping the majority in poverty and distress. For example, in El Salvador the wealthiest two percent, known as the Fourteen Families, has long controlled over half of the farmland, where they produce coffee, cotton, sugar cane, and beef—all exports, not crops to feed the hungry in the country. U.S. military aid in this situation keeps the rich in power and prevents necessary social change.

Food aid is essential in times of famine and disaster, but it can also be harmful. It generally slows down efforts of countries to become self-supporting in food needs. Many times food aid does not reach the people for whom it is given. In Bangladesh, for example, where one third of all food aid comes from the U.S., the World Bank discovered that only a third of the U.S. food aid was distributed in rural areas where 90 percent of the people live; about 27 percent of the food went to police, military, civil servants and employees of large companies; another 30 percent to the middle class in just six major cities.

Where do you see the U.S. transnational corporations fitting into the global economy?

**Bob:** As you have said very clearly, the U.S. needs to keep its economy internationalized in order to sustain its growth. That's its priority.

Transnational corporations (TNCs) are a significant element in the global economic power of the United States. The term transnational refers to the operations, not to ownership of the corporations. Most TNCs operate from industrialized countries. Control of TNCs are in the hands of a relatively few individuals, banks, pension funds, trusts, and insurance companies in the industrialized countries. These few "global managers" have incredible resources at hand. The assets of the 500 largest corporations range from $15 billion to $150 billion. This kind of concentration of money and power in a few hands has a tremendous effect on the global economy. They control technology, can move capital from one country to another, and can threaten to upset the economy of a country by pulling out and relocating in another country which may give them better terms under which to operate. Many of the TNCs have capital turnover larger than and handle more money than many of the sovereign nations. They exert a disproportionate amount of political influence in many developing countries.

The United Nations is trying to work out a code of conduct for the TNCs but is having a difficult time getting the cooperation of the capitalist countries in that effort.

Economists have no doubt about what issues have to be resolved. We face a decade where there will be negotiations on these issues. Now that really means that the majority of the world, who are economically powerless, will have to negotiate with the minority in the world who are the economically powerful. If we have been talking about imbalances before, we are now talking about another major imbalance, a negotiation of the weak with the powerful. I think the 1980s is going to witness the long, painful process of negotiations in which powerful economies, especially the United States, are going to be forced and pressed to share their power.

That puts us in a situation where on the one hand are the powerful trying hard to protect their self-interest in every way possible, and on the other hand are the developing countries, who are tired of being pushed around and are experiencing increasing dissatisfaction and anger. They are frustrated that economic financial decisions affecting them are made without their being included in the decision-making process. Therefore, we have a potential for a collision between the powerful and the powerless. In this decade the various actors will have to try and negotiate on common ground.

**Shantilal:** Do you see signs of a peaceful resolution of the differences between the rich and the poor nations?

**Bob:** I see fewer signs of hopefulness now than I did several years ago. One reason for this is that the Carter Administration, (and I am not an American; therefore I am not partisan about this) was trying, in a very immature way perhaps, to grapple with a long-term view. But, very clearly, the Reagan administration sees the expansion of private investment and the continuing internationalization of the economy as its priority.

**Shantilal:** Pardon me for interrupting, but I disagree with you in your assessment of the Carter administration's policies. I find it difficult to believe that his administration was any more inclined to view economic problems from a long-term perspective than the present administration. The main reason for my skepticism goes back to one of the basic characteristics of the capitalistic economic system. This is that each unit of the economy makes decisions independently of others, keeping in mind its own self-interest, regardless of what is happening in the economy as a whole. The lack of overall coordination and the need to remain solvent in the meanwhile makes a short-term view more practical. That is one of the major difficulties when it comes to dealing with economic problems realistically, both on the U.S. domestic scene as well as internationally.

**Bob:** If you are saying that one of the characteristics of capitalism is to be always short-term in order to bring the maximum profits, then you must be entirely pessimistic about any hope of negotiating between the powerful and the less powerful for the future.

**Shantilal:** That puts it rather strongly. I am not *entirely* pessimistic, although I do have a certain amount of pessimism about the possibilities of major reforms of the economic system. As long as the basic tenet of the system is maximization of profits without adequate consideration for the social costs, I do not see how the system can afford a long-term view or a global view. The cycles of ups and downs, boom and bust, clearly are the outcomes of narrow short-term approaches, designed for quick returns on capital.

My optimism resides in the freedom the political system offers to the citizens of the United States to work for a change. There could be a turnaround if those who are concerned about the economy would do three things. First, they should make a serious attempt to understand the economic system as it operates within the nation and also internationally. Secondly, they should begin to see the inequalities and injustices which are inherent within it. Finally, they should then try to do something to correct the system. These steps are important because, in my opinion, the injustices that are prevalent domestically are also projected internationally.

**Bob:** Are you saying that the main actors in the national economy don't really care about casualties they cause?

**Shantilal:** There is a very small minority who controls the wealth in the United States, and it is their wealth which is invested domestically as well as internationally. A minority controls the future of the majority.

**Bob:** At this point it seems very clear to me that that small minority within the United States and that small minority of rich countries within the international community, are up against the majority of the world. I see the negotiations going on at such international forums as the United Nations, as a nonviolent way of planning the future. There are other ways for planning but they involve bloodshed and war. It disturbs me that the kind of analysis you are offering brings with it war economies; would bring with it militarization in order to sustain power; and yet ignores the insight that basic political stability comes from economic stability.

**Shantilal:** I, too, am disturbed by what I see happening around me. I am concerned about militarism and militarization, the escalating arms race and so forth. History clearly indicates that economics and war are closely linked. Europe blew up in 1848. Why? Because urban misery was intolerable and the promise of new wealth from colonies had not yet brought relief. In 1914 Europe blew up again. Why? Because even the new resources were no longer enough to provide expanding markets and employment for all the competing powers. The world blew up in 1939 after the long depression which spawned Hitler and the Nazis. Who knows where the current global economic situation will land us?

I am also convinced that unless there is a basic change in the thinking of the technologically-oriented, dominant cultures of our globe, our world is headed for a catastrophe of the kind and magnitude never imagined before in human history. And a change is not possible until those in decision-making positions and those in the society as a whole make a connection between private and public ethics and resolve the conflict between the two by shaping a more consistent moral code out of which to operate nationally and globally. The time is here to stop talking about change in the abstract and to take concrete actions toward a global society in which the rights and interests of the least and the lowliest are guarded with the same fervor as those of the big and the powerful.

# 13
# The Economy, Next Steps

The preceding chapters have described our economy and its various components. We have looked at some of the problem areas as well as the structural changes that seem to be taking place in our ever-changing economy. We should now examine the future of our economy. What kind of modifications may be necessary to address its many problems and to meet the needs of the society?

We will not construct a new model, provide a blueprint for an alternative, or spell out specifications for a future society of the United States. Those would be formidable undertakings, not only because of the many complexities of such tasks but also because definitive answers do not yet exist. What we will do is to look at experiments done in several countries, including our own, for clues which may be applicable to the United States.

Let us begin with Europe. A number of programs and proposals for work restructuring that focus on "humanization of work" have been tried in Europe. The humanization of work refers to addressing issues of worker alienation, job dissatisfaction, and stress caused by the changes in work patterns. The new programs have led to movements for "industrial democracy," that is, participation by the workers in the decision-making processes of the company.

Three separate forms of worker participation are identifiable in Europe. The first, introduced in Yugoslavia, is based on nationalized ownership of the means of production. The second, found in Western Europe, is based on a democratic constitution. Ownership in this case is primarily private, although nationalization of a portion of the means of production plays an important role. The third form, used in Sweden, is a type of a welfare state.

### Yugoslavia

Yugoslavia began with the Soviet model of strict central planning and control by the Communist Party, but later changed to a form of market economy. Under the changed situation, the means of production remains nationalized, but a new concept has been introduced. The workers have become the *economic owners* of the business in which they work, but the nation remains the *legal owner* of the means of production.

A work council, elected by workers, sets the policy on matters of production, investment, financing, and distribution of "gain," as well as on how decisions are to be made. The executive committee elected by the work council implements the policies. The director of the enterprise, elected by the workers, works with the staff to make major decisions.

Rewards are based on a low minimum wage plus profit sharing. If losses are so high that even the minimum wage cannot be paid, the surrounding community has to make up the difference. The workers do not have the authority to dispose of the enterprise.

Despite problems, like lack of an overarching national coordination of the economy, high inflation rate, and unemployment, Yugoslavia's economy seems to be more efficient than the economies of the Soviet Union or its satellites. In addition, the workers and other citizens have political rights.

### Western Europe

In Western Europe, two forms of worker participation

have emerged. The first takes the form of a work council advisory committee composed of labor and management. The functions of this committee vary from serving as a communication channel to dealing with specific programs like welfare, shop programming, and shop planning or profit-sharing planning. The second form of worker participation is at the level of the board of directors. In the Federal Republic of Germany, legislation had been enacted which gave labor the right to elect one third to one half of a firm's supervisory board. Norway has legislation which requires companies with more than two hundred employees to institute a Board of Representatives composed of one-third employees and two-thirds stockholders.

Overall, the experience in Western Europe has been positive so long as worker participation is related to basic problems and management retains the authority to make the final decisions. Whether workers should participate in long-term decision making or in management-type decision making, however, is more controversial.

### Sweden

In Sweden, cooperative communities date back to 1946. In 1965, modern work councils were formally introduced by a collective bargaining between the national confederations of unions and employees. The responsibility of the work councils was to work for increased productivity and work satisfaction.

Workers also participate at the level of the board of directors. The workers co-determine, along with the shareholders, the direction a company takes. Sweden also has worker representation on the firm's supervisory board which works on the humanizing of the workplace.

Although Sweden is referred to as a welfare state, it is unmistakably capitalist in its economic structure. About 85 percent of the industry is privately owned. Industry is highly concentrated within fifteen or twenty corporations, many of them family-owned. The ownership is even more concentrated than in the United States.

Sweden, however, has adopted what has been known as the "middle way" in economic life, introducing into its capitalist productive mechanism an element of socialism, that is, a concern for social equality and well being. For example, when a Swedish working class couple have a baby, they are entitled to seven months of parental benefits at 90 percent of the income they would otherwise earn. These benefits begin one month before delivery. After the baby is born, these benefits may be claimed by either mother or father, depending on how they decide the child's care between them.

The child's health, education, and retirement benefits are generally covered. Health benefits include all conventional medical and hospital costs, and even include reimbursement of travel costs for certain types of health care. Dental care is also heavily subsidized.

Generous retirement benefits for everyone, and other forward-looking policies for workers have placed the label "socialism" on the Swedish welfare state. It is important to note, however, that the most socialist aspect is not its emphasis on income distribution, but rather, the rights the workers have earned on the factory floor and in the management sphere. Strong unions—90 percent of the blue-collar workers and 70 percent of the white-collar workers are union members—have succeeded in influencing the economy in favor of the workers.

How are the social expenditures financed in Sweden? Corporate income taxes produce only a tiny fraction of the revenue the Swedish government gets from individuals. The U.S. treasury collects about one dollar from corporations for every three dollars it collects from individuals. In Sweden, it is more like one to ten. The Swedes have chosen to divert a big share of their national income into investments and to finance their welfare state through heavy personal taxes, sometimes running up to 60 or 70 percent of incomes.

The Swedish economy, like other capitalist economies, has been undergoing a period of trial. After four decades, the expanding welfare state seems to have lost momentum. Despite the uncertainty surrounding the loss of economic, social, and political momentum, the Swedish model is worth looking at.

*Experiments in America*

The "industrial democracy" movement portends a significant change in the economic structure of Europe. It is anticipated that by the end of this decade every country in Europe (excluding Eastern European countries) will have obligatory legislations reqiring corporate enterprises to practice some form of industrial democracy.

The growth of the movement in Europe may largely be due to the support of the government, labor, and management and perhaps because of Europe's predominantly socialist character. Whether or not they grow, or even survive, these developments offer a great deal for American business to think about. However, the U.S. system is different, the labor unions are different, and democracy is different. Therefore, the model for our economic transformation will have to be a distinctly American product, growing out of our own history and culture.

Although the European experiments in worker participation in management have not received much attention in the United States, a steadily growing movement for self-management by workers has beeen gaining ground in this country. With the changing character of the labor force (younger workers, better educated workers, more women and black and other minorities), experiments in the quality of life in the workplace and in work democracy are bound to grow and be accepted. While labor unions are the driving force for innovations in workplace democracy in Europe, in the United States, by contrast, most organizational innovations come from management.

An example of management-initiated innovation is found

in the General Foods Gravy Train plant in Topeka, Kansas, which began operation in 1971. The plant was designed to allow employees a considerable degree of freedom in operating the production process. The general idea was that workers could do whatever they wanted as long as the dog food was produced. The production was structured so that there were about 123 jobs and workers rotated among the jobs. Workers were paid according to how many different jobs they learned. Those who could do different jobs earned more. Very quickly, workers understood all the jobs, from unloading materials to running the dog food ingredients through the mixer and processor, to chemical analysis for quality control, to packaging and loading the finished product. Production increased with minimum supervision by managers, and workers had time off if they finished early.

Over the years, problems seem to have developed in the Topeka plant, but it is an example of possibilities for "humanization" of work, workers' control, and self-management.

Some 5,000 businesses are operated under employee stock ownership plans in the United States and, increasingly, as industrial plants have closed, such plans are gaining ground. A recent example of this trend is found in Clark, N.J., where workers bought the General Motors corporation's plant manufacturing bearings for automobiles and railroads, when GM decided to close it down. It is now called Hyatt-Clark Industries, Inc. The new company is trying innovations like equal distribution of stock and bonuses; white-collar and blue-collar employees working together to improve the company; a twenty-five-member employee committee to help iron out problems and train supervisors, and so on.

Community living has been a common experience throughout history and our age is no exception to it. Rosebeth Kanter observes that contemporary communes began as religious or politico-economic critiques of society, but underneath they were the product of a reaction against the detrimental byproducts (e.g., alienation, loneliness) of modern civilization. Seeking relief from social isolation and inner fragmentation, some people have turned to communes, not only to get back in touch with others but also to get in touch with their inner selves.

Communes are innovative and they experiment with new forms of social organization. Up to the present, American communes have not provided much change to society at large, but the kibbutz movement in Israel is an example of how a commune movement can become a significant political force by working closely with the rest of the society. Given the right kind of environment and scale of operation, the commune movement in the U.S. has the potential to become a powerful force for societal change.

A cooperative approach in a variety of spheres of life merits serious consideration by Christians and others alike. A model of this approach is the Amish community, which has survived the onslaught of modern civilization in the U.S. since the 1700s and has now an estimated 85,000 adherents. Another area for exploration is the area of "small is beautiful" and the movement for appropriate technology in the era of "bigger is better" and of high technology.

We have seen that income and wealth distribution are very uneven in our society. Highly consolidated personal wealth and huge amounts of bank-controlled, institutionally-owned wealth together represent a tremendous concentration of economic, and therefore political, power in a few hands. As we begin to look for ways to reform our economic system without totally destroying it, several possibilities come to mind.

One important area to explore is that segment of our wealth which is represented in pension funds. Although pension funds eventually benefit the workers, they are mostly managed and controlled by banks and other financial institutions. Therefore, even though pension funds (both private and public) totaled $611.1 billion in 1979, they did not present a source of power for workers in the same sense that personal wealth is a source of power to capital owners.

Two other funds into which working households pour their savings are savings bank deposits and insurance reserves. In 1979 these two together totaled $915.1 billion and all three funds amounted to a pool of $1,537.2 billion, representing an enormous leverage. Workers' control of investment of these funds could make a lot of difference as to how our economy is shaped.

Another important area for the possibility of a democratic reform is our tax system. Does our tax system fulfill our understanding of the concept of economic justice? Should we have a severe inheritance tax system to guard against inter-generational transfers of undue concentrations of wealth? These vastly unequal starting points are unjust and laden with the potential of putting wrong persons in leadership positions. Should we favor replacement of the present income tax system with a consumption tax that would tax borrowings used to finance consumption so as to encourage savings for investment and discourage consumption? There are other kinds of taxes like payroll taxes, corporate taxes, sales and property taxes, and so on, about which similar questions could be raised.

The question of property rights and property ownership assumes great importance, particularly at this juncture in our history. A few capital owners wield a disproportionate amount of power in our economy and their decisions affect the lives of millions of workers. Thousands of communities are affected by plant closings, relocation or flight of capital. Is it ethical to accept the right of private ownership of property as an absolute right? Or should certain responsibilities and restrictions be accepted as a part of "private" ownership of property? Often the consequences of unrestricted private ownership are quite public, and that right ceases to serve a useful social function, but instead, causes suffering and controls the lives and futures of other human beings.

Some American socialist thinkers would propose a version of socialism as an alternative to capitalism. They look to no foreign model as appropriate for the United States but expect a model to evolve as workers struggle for a better life within the context of our own history, culture, and developments of the past. The vision includes both economic and political democracy which would give individuals the right and duty to structure their lives through direct participatory control. Many of their goals are worth consideration even though their program may not be acceptable without modification.

Among the goals of the socialist vision are the development of an alternative wage-labor system. Such a system would plan for a progressive democratization of the workplace, and guarantee food, shelter, medical care, and social services to everyone irrespective of their economic position in society. They also seek to make political life progressively democratic by steps such as

• local, regional, and national planning for production,
• the organization of social services,
• determining what the consumption needs are,
• assigning a significant role to the national government for a coordinated, balanced, and equal development at local and regional levels,
• abolition of the private ownership of capital and the means of production to bring about true political democracy through an economic democracy. A redistribution of wealth is included in this goal in order to provide an equal access for all to material and cultural resources.

These goals are based upon a conviction that only a new social order with social institutions that meet people's needs can solve the problems of an advanced capitalist society of the United States.

Obtaining power through a peaceful revolution which promotes democracy, participation, and a sense of solidarity and equality is the aim of the socialists. However, they expect to meet strong opposition, even violence, from those whose power they challenge.

Management, labor, government, and academia look at our economy and draw different conclusions about its future. Some think our capitalistic economic system, with its shortcomings, is still the best in the world and needs no change. Others believe that, while our economic system is not perfect, it can evolve and adapt if its basic framework is preserved and strengthened. There are also those who are convinced that the system is beyond reform and should be scrapped for a new system. Some say a substitution of public for private ownership of the means of production would solve our problems. Others advocate a democratic, decentralized system in which people participate in making decisions which affect their lives. Be that as it may, there are no easy alternatives.

*The Role of the Church*

We are a part of our economic system, of industrial capitalism. It is through our involvement with this system that most of us receive our rewards and experience our limitations. As Christians we value justice which deals with the way in which the major social institutions (e.g. the political constitution and the principal economic and social arrangements) distribute fundamental rights and duties and determine the divisions of advantages from social cooperation.

Christians have a biblical mandate to do justice. The Bible places justice squarely within the righteous will of the living God who creates, rules, and redeems the world. God calls people into a covenant community. Without justice the covenant is betrayed. Justice in biblical thought is also linked to compassion, with compassionate caring. Such caring is a response to a rightful claim by the neighbor as well as God's claim. Caring is not an optional charitable contribution.

What is the meaning of justice? Justice is the social principle that all human beings have certain basic needs and an

essentially equal right to share in the resources necessary for
the satisfaction of these needs. All human beings have a
rightful claim upon the means of life and fulfillment. A society
is just only when its laws, structures, and systems embody a
concern for all its members and acknowledge the value of every
individual. Justice requires a society where all persons can obtain the necessities of life and enhance the possibilities
available for a fulfilling life. To a very large extent, it is
primarily in the sphere of economics that such arrangements
have to be achieved.

In economics, justice focuses sharply upon the equitable
distribution of available goods and services. Justice, therefore,
means distributive justice, that is, the entire question of the
proper distribution of goods and services within the society.
Distributive justice is the principle of fairness applied to the
availability of the ingredients required for a reasonably secure
and fulfilling life. Distributive justice is an integral part of the
meaning of love of neighbor. It is an unavoidable implication
of the solidarity of God's human creatures. It includes, along
with other things, the arrangements for an equitable distribution of goods and services needed by all members of the
community.

The faithful Christian or church seeks justice in a world
that remains in bondage to the forces of injustice. Although
perfect justice is found only in the kingdom of God, we have to
be faithful in this world and join God in bringing about as
much justice as possible through the societal structures. If I
see my brother or sister in need, I am commanded to share the
goods I have. This also means to engage in the task of fashion-
ing an economic system wherein sufficient food shall be
distributed to all; wherein jobs are available to everyone who
wants work; and wherein the basic needs of each and every
child of God are met, irrespective of whether or not persons are
gainfully employed or can be employed.

Does the Bible have a model for us which can help us to go

about the task of achieving social justice? Perhaps, we have a model in Amos of Tekoa, the first Hebrew prophet who founded the prophetic tradition which Jesus took as his own. The era in which Amos addressed his brief but powerful ministry to the religious and political powers of Israel has many parallels with our own. Amos found extremes of riches and poverty, deceitful business practices, expropriation of land of small landowners and so on. Today the injustices of Israel's early capitalism addressed by Amos are being replicated on a global scale by industrial capitalism.

God shook Amos loose from his day to day routine of raising sheep and taking care of sycamore trees and asked him, "Go, prophesy to my people." God says the same thing to us today, "Go, prophesy." In the same way God asked Amos, God calls us away from following the flock and holds human suffering and human hope before us and asks us to "Go, prophesy."

The life of Jesus reveals even more vividly human suffering and the message of hope. Whether one looks at the message of Jesus to the rich young ruler, "Go and sell all that you have and give to the poor," or at the example of Zacchaeus, who gave half of his goods to the poor and promised to restore fourfold any money which had been fraudulently taken, or at the example of the early church which "had all things in common," the New Testament witness is the same. Paul's advice to the church at Corinth was "I do not mean that others should be eased and you burdened, but that as a matter of equality your abundance at the present time should supply their want, so that their abundance may supply your want that there may be equality." (2 Cor. 8:13-14 ). Yet is it a curious fact that the Protestant ethic of the nineteenth century and the Protestant Church largely ignored the greatest upheaval of social life in the modern world; the rise and victorious expansion of capitalistic economics.

God calls us to work and witness, but we have built defenses against admitting that the basis of our social ministry rests in God's own special call. Could this be because our inward spiritual life is poor? Can we carry out our social ministry and social action without creating an uncluttered interior space for God out of which we can live and work? It is prayer and devotion which help us in creating such space within ourselves. Without cultivating this inner space we cannot be empowered to act for justice from an inner peace and quiet and a sense of grounding in God. If we operate out of an inner peace, we will not be concerned about the future but will confront the injustices trusting that the principalities and powers have been defeated and only need our assistance to make them disappear from the scene. Our action thus flows, not out of an overcrowded, angry, and harassed interior, but out of a space we have allowed God to create within us, which in turn permits us to absorb the sufferings which the many injustices and inequities leave in their trail.

Often, we are tempted to keep our faith and politics separate. Can we really do that in these times? We live in a complex world in which politics, economics, and religion cannot be neatly separated. As heirs to the Judeo-Christian tradition and as men and women of faith, we believe in the sovereignty of God and in the biblical teachings of justice and liberty. Moses, Gideon, Jeremiah, Amos, and Jesus—all these were involved in the struggle to set people free from bondage for primarily religious reasons. Therefore, if we divorce that dynamic faith from politics in our day, we have stepped outside the biblical tradition. If faith does not determine our political stance today, then we have adopted for ourselves a religion that does not exalt Jesus. We have forsaken his teachings of justice and the solidarity of all peoples. Let us, therefore, search together how to respond to the many dilemmas we, as Christians, face within our industrial capitalistic economic system.